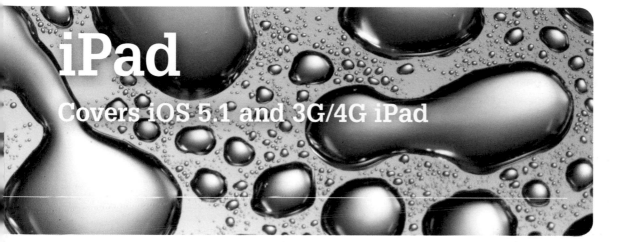

iPad

Covers iOS 5.1 and 3G/4G iPad

in Simple steps

Marc Campbell

Use your computer with confidence

Get to grips with practical computing tasks with minimal time, fuss and bother.

In Simple Steps guides guarantee immediate results. They tell you everything you need to know on a specific application; from the most essential tasks to master, to every activity you'll want to accomplish, through to solving the most common problems you'll encounter.

Helpful features

To build your confidence and help you to get the most out of your iPad, practical hints, tips and shortcuts feature on every page:

ALERT: Explains and provides practical solutions to the most commonly encountered problems

HOT TIP: Time and effort saving shortcuts

SEE ALSO: Points you to other related tasks and information

DID YOU KNOW? Additional features to explore

WHAT DOES THIS MEAN?
Jargon and technical terms explained in plain English

Practical. Simple. Fast.

in **Simple** steps

Acknowledgements

These people provided simple instructions that I kept finding reasons not to follow, so please join me in thanking them for their kindness and patience as well as their professional expertise: Neil Salkind, Andrew Kim, Ken Bluttman, Steve Temblett, Robert Cottee, Helen Savill, Linda Dhondy and Joli Ballew, not to mention the unsung heroes in production and elsewhere, including the marketing department.

I'm also extremely grateful to my friends who agreed to appear in the examples, namely OJ at nomadbuzz.com, Wendy at www.createawaytoday.com and David at davidfedan.blogspot.com. Billy Blind appears courtesy of no one in particular.

Publisher's acknowledgements

The publisher would like to thank the following for their kind permission to include their photographs within screenshots on the following pages:

Page 181 (bottom) Pearson Education Ltd; page 184 Pearson Education Ltd; page 185 Pearson Education Ltd: Photodisc. Kevin Peterson; page 186 Pearson Education Ltd; page 188 Pearson Education Ltd; page 190 Pearson Education Ltd.

Every effort has been made to trace the copyright holders and we apologise in advance for any unintentional omissions. We would be pleased to insert the appropriate acknowledgement in any subsequent edition of this publication.

in Simple steps

Contents at a glance

Top 10 iPad Problems Solved

Contents

Top 10 iPad Tips

1 Hello iPad!

2 Setting up your iPad

3 Shopping for music, movies and apps

4 Surfing the Web with Safari

11 Getting oriented with Maps

12 Caring for your contacts

16 Getting more out of Settings

Top 10 iPad Problems Solved

Top Ten iPad Tips

Tip 1: Dictate instead of type

If you'd rather speak your thoughts aloud instead of typing them, you can dictate to your iPad whenever you see the virtual keyboard. The iPad inserts your speech as text. To use this feature, you must have an active Internet connection.

1 When you see the virtual keyboard, tap the key with the microphone icon. You can find this key to the left of the spacebar.

2 Speak the text that you want to type. A volume meter appears above the dictation key, so that you can see that the iPad is capturing your voice.

3 Tap the key with the microphone icon again. After a moment, your speech appears as text at the cursor.

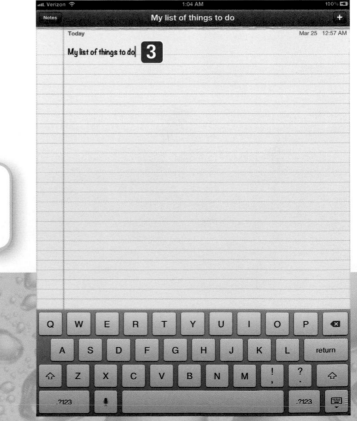

? DID YOU KNOW?

To disable or enable the dictation feature, look under Settings > General > Keyboard > Dictation.

HOT TIP: To insert a punctuation mark, pronounce the name of the punctuation mark.

Tip 2: Set up iCloud

Your iPad can connect to Apple's iCloud service, which stores your music, mail, photos, and other kinds of data online. The main advantage to using iCloud is that you can share your data among devices without the bother of hooking up cables. For example, if you download some music from iTunes on your iPad and you want to listen to it on your computer, you don't need to connect the iPad to the computer. The iCloud service simply goes ahead and copies (or pushes) the music to the computer – and any other iCloud device that uses your account. All the devices must have Internet access, but they don't need to be online simultaneously. You get 5GB of iCloud storage for free, but you can always buy more if you need it, and the content and apps that you purchase from Apple's stores don't count towards your storage limit.

1 In Settings, tap iCloud. If you want to use an existing Apple ID or create a new Apple ID to associate with iCloud, tap the appropriate button, and work through the screens that follow.

2 The iCloud settings screen shows On/Off switches for various kinds of data, including mail, contacts and calendars, among others. Tap the switch to engage or disengage iCloud for this type of data.

3 Set up your computer and other devices to work with iCloud. For step-by-step instructions for each of your devices, go to www.apple.com/icloud/get-started/.

4 To review your data in the cloud, log in to www.icloud.com on a computer.

? DID YOU KNOW?

You can use iCloud to help you locate a misplaced iPad! Make sure to engage this feature under iCloud in your iPad settings. Then, to locate your iPad, sign in at www.icloud.com and choose Find My iPad.

Tip 3: Set up an email account

Using your iPad for email is a no-brainer. You can even set up multiple email accounts.

1 In Settings, tap the Mail, Contacts, Calendars item.

2 In the list of options that appears, tap to add an account.

3 Select an email provider. You may already have an email account with one of these providers. If so, that's fine; you can simply enter your existing information.

4 Fill in the required information. You might need to go through a sequence of screens. When you're finished, tap the Save button.

5 Continue adding as many email accounts as you like.

Tip 4: Rent a movie

Quite a number of iTunes movies are available for rental. When you rent a movie from iTunes, your iPad downloads the movie, but it isn't yours to keep. Instead, you get it for a maximum of 30 days. Once you start watching it, you have 24 hours to finish. You can watch the movie as many times as you like over this 24-hour window, but afterwards, your rental is done, even if you watch it before your 30 days are over.

1 Find the movie that you want to rent, and tap the Rent button, which shows the price for the rental.

2 The price changes to the Rent Movie confirmation message. Tap this button. If you aren't already logged in, the iTunes Store asks you to enter your Apple ID and password.

3 To prevent unauthorised rentals, the iTunes Store might ask for the password of your Apple ID. Type it in the field, and tap OK to start the download.

4 Once the download finishes, press the Home button, and then tap the Videos icon to watch your rental. Remember, once you start watching it, you have 24 hours to finish, and don't wait longer than 30 days to start.

HOT TIP: You can rent some movies in high definition (HD) or standard definition (SD). Make sure to select the version that you want before you start tapping prices.

ALERT: When you rent a movie from your iPad, you must watch it on your iPad. You can't transfer the rental to another device the way you might with media that you purchase from iTunes.

Tip 5: Create a Home icon to navigate directly to a website

When you launch Safari from the Safari icon, you start from the site that you visited last. But if you launch Safari from a custom Home icon, you begin directly in the site of your choosing.

1 In Safari, navigate to the desired website.

2 Tap the icon for options, which appears to the left of the address field. A menu appears.

3 Tap Add to Home Screen.

4 In the Add to Home box that opens, type a name for the icon, or use the name that Safari supplies by default.

5 Tap Add. Safari adds the icon for this site to your Home screen.

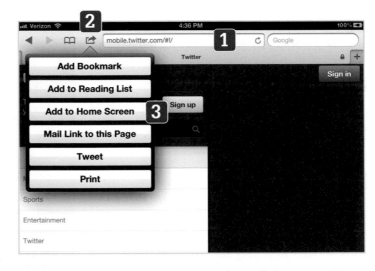

? DID YOU KNOW?

You can set up as many of these website shortcut icons as you like.

Tip 6: Make video calls with FaceTime

Text messages are great, but wouldn't you rather be chatting face to face? With the FaceTime app, you can do just that. FaceTime connects with any other FaceTime user over Wi-Fi. When you make a call, you get video and audio of your recipient, and they get video and audio of you. Of course, the devices on either end of the call need three things: the FaceTime app, a camera and a microphone. Your iPad has all three, as do newer iPhones and Mac computers.

1 From the Home screen, tap FaceTime. Your iPad launches the FaceTime app.

2 Tap the Contacts button at the lower right of the screen.

3 Choose a contact to call from the list that appears.

4 In the Info box that appears, tap the contact's mobile phone number or email address. FaceTime attempts to start a video call with this contact. If the connection succeeds, the call begins.

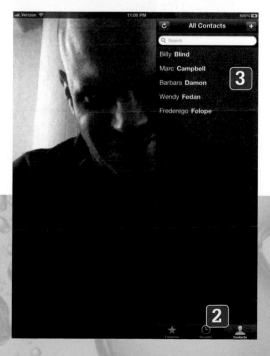

HOT TIP: You can also choose a person to call from your Favorites and Recents lists, which appear when you tap the Favorites and Recents buttons at the bottom of the screen.

5 To mute the audio from your microphone, tap the microphone icon. Tap the icon again to unmute the audio.

6 To switch from your iPad's front camera to the back camera, tap the camera icon.

7 To end the call, tap End.

Tip 7: Take a photo with your iPad

For those times when someone tells you, 'Take a picture; it'll last longer,' your iPad comes with a built-in digital camera. The default lens is on the back, in the upper left corner (or the upper right corner when you're looking at the screen). You use the Camera app to take the photos, which go to your Camera Roll and, if you're on iCloud, they also go into your Photo Stream for distribution to all your iCloud devices.

1 From the Home screen, tap Camera. The Camera app launches.

2 Hold your iPad so that the lens on the back points towards your subject. The screen shows what the lens sees. To zoom in on your subject, use the pinch gesture.

3 Tap the round button with the camera icon on the right side of the screen to take a picture.

! ALERT: The Camera app uses Location Services to determine your location. If you don't want to include location information in the photos that you take, make sure that you disengage Location Services for the Camera app under Settings > Location Services.

HOT TIP: If you want to take a picture with the lens on the front of your iPad – the one that you use for Photo Booth and FaceTime – tap the button with the camera icon and two curved arrows, which you find at the bottom of the screen towards the right.

? DID YOU KNOW?
You can use the Camera app to shoot video, too. In Camera, find the Camera/Video switch in the lower right corner, and tap it to alternate between still photos and videos.

Tip 8: Listen to music while using another app

One of the great things about the Music app is that it doesn't need to appear onscreen in order for you to listen to audio. In fact, if you exit Music while audio is playing, the audio continues to play no matter what you're doing on your iPad, unless you need sound for some other feature (like playing a movie). You can even pause playback and skip or repeat audio selections without going back into Music.

1 Launch the Music app, and get some music playing.

⚫⚫⚫						
Artists	Ben Harper and the Innocent Criminals					
	Burn to Shine				**1999**	
	1.	Alone			3:59	
	2.	The Woman in You			5:42	
	3.	Less			4:06	
	4.	Two Hands of a Prayer			7:51	
	5.	Please Bleed			4:38	
	6.	Suzie Blue			4:30	
	7.	Steal My Kisses			4:06	
	8.	Burn to Shine			3:35	
	9.	Show Me a Little Shame			3:45	
	10.	Forgiven			5:18	
	11.	Beloved One			4:04	
	12.	In the Lord's Arms			3:07	
	Live from Mars [Disc 1]				**2001**	
	1.	Glory & Consequence			6:02	
	2.	Excuse Me Mr.			4:55	
	3.	Alone			5:01	
	4.	Sexual Healing			5:15	
	5.	Woman in You			8:01	
	6.	Ground On Down			5:40	
	7.	Steal My Kisses			5:16	
	8.	Burn One Down			4:54	

Store Playlists Songs Artists Albums More Harper

2 Press the Home button. The Music app closes, but the music keeps playing. You're free to use your iPad however you like. To get back into Music, tap its icon.

3 To show playback controls from any app, press the Home button twice in quick succession. A bar of recent apps appears along the bottom of the screen.

4 Flick this bar to the right to see the playback controls. Use them, and then press the Home button again to hide them.

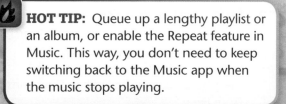

HOT TIP: Queue up a lengthy playlist or an album, or enable the Repeat feature in Music. This way, you don't need to keep switching back to the Music app when the music stops playing.

Tip 9: Get directions to anywhere from anywhere

The Maps app's Directions mode gives you turn-by-turn directions for finding almost any location. If you want to use your iPad's current location as the starting point, make sure that you've enabled Location Services for Maps; see 'Find your location on the map' in Chapter 11 for more information.

1 In Maps, tap the Directions button at the top of the interface.

2 Tap the field for the starting location, and enter the address or place-name of your starting point. Choose *Current Location* (if necessary) to use your iPad's current coordinates.

3 Tap the destination field, and then type the address or name of the destination. You don't need to be exact; you can type the name of a town or city, but doing so limits your ability to find a specific house on a specific street.

4 Tap Search on the keyboard. Maps computes a route between the points.

ALERT: The Maps app's directions don't take into account detours, recent construction, and so on. Always defer to traffic signs and the conditions on the road if you receive contradictory information.

DID YOU KNOW?
Another way to get directions is to search for a location, tap its pin, tap the blue information button that appears, and then tap Directions To Here or Directions From Here.

5 Near the bottom of the interface, find a bar of controls for the mode of transport: by car, by public transportation, or by walking. The default is by car. Tap any other mode to get a new route.

6 If you're using public transportation, tap the button with the clock icon to choose your transit times.

7 Tap the Start button.

8 Go through the legs of the journey step by step by tapping the arrow buttons on the right side of the bar. To return to the controls for the modes of transport, tap the left-arrow button until you return to the first leg of the journey, and then tap the left arrow one more time.

HOT TIP: To view the directions as a list, tap the button on the left of the bar. Tap the icon at the top left of the Directions box to close the list.

HOT TIP: To reverse the directions, tap the button with the wavy arrow between the fields for the starting and ending locations.

Tip 10: Set an alert to remind you of an event

Calendar is great for keeping you organised. But on days when your schedule looks like air traffic control, Calendar by itself might not be enough. If you'd prefer a friendly reminder that a can't-miss engagement is coming up, Calendar can double as your personal assistant. When the time arrives for the alert, Calendar plays a sound, and you see a text reminder on the screen.

1 Add or edit an event, and tap the Alert button in the Add Event or Edit box.

2 In the list of choices that appears, choose when Calendar should alert you about the event.

3 Tap Done. The display reverts to the Add Event or Edit box.

HOT TIP: You can change the sound of the alert under Options > General > Sounds > Calendar Alerts.

4 Notice the Second Alert option; tap it to set a second reminder, and then tap Done. For example, you can set the first alert to 15 minutes before the event and the second reminder to 5 minutes before.

5 Tap Done in the Add Event or Edit box.

1 Hello iPad!

Introduction

If you're new to the world of tablet computing, you might be wondering where your iPad keeps all its buttons. There are very few controls on the iPad itself, since you access its features and tools primarily through the touch-sensitive screen. But if you look closely, you'll find various parts, switches and connectors tucked away around the rim, including: a headphone jack; a microphone; the On/Off, Sleep/Wake button; the side switch (for locking the display rotation or muting sound effects); the volume control; a speaker; the dock connector; optionally, the micro-SIM card tray (for connecting to a cellular data network).

The front of the iPad features the Home button and the screen, not to mention a camera lens; there's another camera lens on the back.

The iPad comes loaded with a number of applications or *apps*: Spotlight (the search feature); Messages; Calendar; Notes; Reminders; Maps; YouTube; Videos; Contacts; Game Center; iTunes; App Store; Newsstand; FaceTime; Camera; Photo Booth; Settings; Safari; Mail; Photos; Music.

Some of the apps require a connection to the Internet. The iPad can go online through either Wi-Fi or a high-speed cellular data network, including HSPA, HSPA+ and DC-HSDPA. If you visit the United States or Canada (and insert the appropriate micro-SIM card), the iPad can play on certain 4G and LTE networks, too. Unfortunately, 4G networks outside North America will operate on bands incompatible with the iPad, so if you want to take advantage of 4G speeds, you'll probably need to wait for the next generation of iPad (which shouldn't be more than a year away).

Turn your iPad on and off

Your iPad might look fantastic, but it doesn't do very much until you turn it on.

1 Press down and hold the On/Off, Sleep/Wake button until the Apple logo appears.

2 The Apple logo remains on the screen until the iPad is ready for use, which can take a few moments.

3 To turn your iPad off, hold the On/Off, Sleep/Wake button until the Shutdown screen appears. Drag the Slide to Power Off slider all the way to the right to complete the shutdown process.

? DID YOU KNOW?

Your iPad has an in-between state called Sleep mode for conserving battery power. In Sleep mode, the screen goes dark, but the iPad is still running, and after you wake it up and unlock it, you simply resume what you were doing. You can put the iPad to sleep yourself by pressing and releasing the On/Off, Sleep/Wake button, or you can wait for the iPad to put itself to sleep after a few minutes of inactivity. To wake up your iPad, press the On/Off, Sleep/Wake button again, or press the Home button. Then unlock your iPad by dragging the slider that appears.

Recharge your iPad's battery

When you take your iPad out into the world with you, it runs on power from its internal battery. You get about 9–10 hours of standard usage before you must recharge. The best way to do this is to plug your iPad into an electric socket using the cable and AC adaptor that came from the factory.

1 Connect the wider, flatter end of the cable to the dock connector on the iPad.

2 Plug the thinner, longer end of the cable into the AC adaptor.

3 Plug the AC adaptor into an electric socket, and your iPad begins to charge. You can tell the current charge level of the battery by looking for the battery icon in the upper right corner of the screen. Feel free to use the iPad while it's charging.

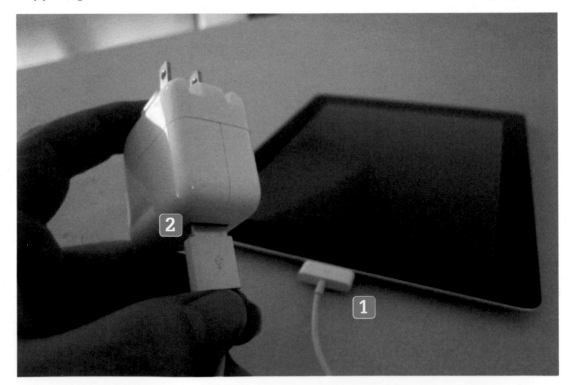

HOT TIP: When you're using your iPad at home and indoors, try to keep it plugged into an electric socket. This way, your battery has the highest possible charge for when you need to go mobile.

? DID YOU KNOW?
You use the same cable to charge the iPad and connect the iPad to a computer.

Use the touch screen

The iPad's screen is touch-sensitive, and it responds to a variety of actions or *gestures*.

1 Use the *tap* gesture to launch an app, activate a button or flip a switch. Think of it like a mouse click. To tap, press on the screen and release.

2 Use the *swipe* gesture to scroll through a list of choices or push an app off the screen. To swipe, brush the screen with one or more fingers.

3 Use the *pinch* gesture to zoom in or zoom out. To pinch, place two fingers on the screen and move them towards each other (or move them farther apart).

HOT TIP: To exit the current app, press the Home button just below the screen.

? DID YOU KNOW?

Each gesture has a number of variations that often produce different results. For example, tapping, double-tapping or holding your finger down on the screen might select, zoom in or open a menu, depending on the context. If it all seems hopelessly complex, don't worry. You'll get the hang of it with practice.

Use the virtual keyboard

Whenever you need to enter text, the iPad displays a virtual keyboard along the bottom of the screen. To type, simply tap the keys.

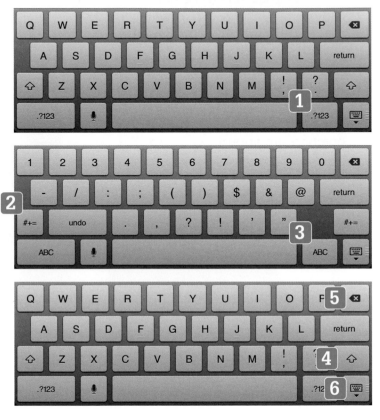

1 The virtual keyboard usually appears with most of the keys representing letters. To show the keys for numbers and typographical symbols, tap the .?123 key.

2 To show the keys for additional symbols, tap the #+= key.

3 To revert to the keys for letters, tap the ABC key.

4 To simulate the SHIFT key on a keyboard, tap the key with the up arrow. The SHIFT automatically turns itself off after the next key that you tap, unless you double-tap the up arrow to engage SHIFT LOCK. Double-tap the up arrow again to release SHIFT LOCK.

5 To simulate the BACKSPACE key on a keyboard, tap the key on the far right of the first row.

6 To hide the virtual keyboard, tap the key at the bottom right of the keyboard.

HOT TIP: To type a character with an accent, hold down your finger on the associated letter key until a menu of character variations appears. Slide your finger to the desired character, and release.

Dictate instead of type

If you'd rather speak your thoughts aloud instead of typing them, you can dictate to your iPad whenever you see the virtual keyboard. The iPad inserts your speech as text. To use this feature, you must have an active Internet connection.

1 When you see the virtual keyboard, tap the key with the microphone icon. You can find this key to the left of the spacebar.

2 Speak the text that you want to type. A volume meter appears above the dictation key, so that you can see that the iPad is capturing your voice.

3 Tap the key with the microphone icon again. After a moment, your speech appears as text at the cursor.

HOT TIP: To insert a punctuation mark, pronounce the name of the punctuation mark.

? DID YOU KNOW?

To disable or enable the dictation feature, look under Settings > General > Keyboard > Dictation.

Rotate the display

No matter which way you hold your iPad, the iPad rotates the display so that you can see what you're doing (and reading).

1 To rotate the display to Landscape mode, hold the iPad so that the screen is wider than it is tall.

2 To rotate the display to Portrait mode, hold the iPad so that the screen is taller than it is wide.

HOT TIP: To prevent your iPad from rotating the display, choose Settings > General, and tap Lock Rotation under Use Side Switch To. Then simply engage the side switch on the right side of your iPad.

Use the Settings app

The settings and options for your iPad itself as well as the apps that run on it appear in an app called Settings, which works like a control panel. Many's the time that this book will tell you to 'go into Settings' or 'look under Settings'; this is what it's talking about.

1 From the Home screen, tap the Settings icon.

2 The list on the left organises settings and options into categories. Tap the category that you wish to review.

3 Make your selections on the right side of the screen. Depending on what you tap on the left, the choices on the right might open menus or screens with further options.

HOT TIP: Apps that you download from the Apps Store might also appear as Settings categories. Tap an app's entry to open the options.

Join a Wi-Fi network

A Wi-Fi network is a wireless network that gives you access to the Internet. You might have one set up in your home, or you might find one in your favourite coffee bar. Your iPad senses nearby Wi-Fi networks and enables you to join them. Some Wi-Fi networks are open to all, while others require a WEP identifier, which works like a password. If you see a network with a lock icon in the list of available networks, you need to supply the correct password before you can join.

1 In Settings, tap Wi-Fi.

2 In the list of options on the right, check that Wi-Fi is engaged. If it isn't, tap the On/Off switch.

3 Select a Wi-Fi network to connect to.

4 If the network requires a WEP identifier, a box appears for you to enter the password.

? DID YOU KNOW?

Wi-Fi networks have a rather short range, which makes them convenient when you're sitting in one place but next to useless when you're travelling. If you need Internet access on the go, you should sign up for a cellular data plan, as long as your iPad is capable of connecting to a cellular service.

Join a cellular data network

Signing up for a cellular data service enables you to connect to the Internet as you would with a smartphone. This option is available on some but not all iPad models.

1 In Settings, tap Cellular Data.

2 In the list of options on the right, check that Cellular Data is engaged. If it isn't, tap the On/Off switch.

3 Tap View Account. A box appears for you to set up your account.

4 Follow the onscreen instructions to choose and set up a data plan.

5 After you have entered your information, the provider sets up your new account. This process might take a couple minutes. Your iPad alerts you when your new account is active.

HOT TIP: Use your finger to scroll through screens if necessary.

Set up iCloud

Your iPad can connect to Apple's iCloud service, which stores your music, mail, photos, and other kinds of data online. The main advantage to using iCloud is that you can share your data among devices without the bother of hooking up cables. For example, if you download some music from iTunes on your iPad and you want to listen to it on your computer, you don't need to connect the iPad to the computer. The iCloud service simply goes ahead and copies (or pushes) the music to the computer – and any other iCloud device that uses your account. All the devices must have Internet access, but they don't need to be online simultaneously. You get 5GB of iCloud storage for free, but you can always buy more if you need it, and the content and apps that you purchase from Apple's stores don't count towards your storage limit.

1 In Settings, tap iCloud. If you want to use an existing Apple ID or create a new Apple ID to associate with iCloud, tap the appropriate button, and work through the screens that follow.

2 The iCloud settings screen shows On/Off switches for various kinds of data, including mail, contacts and calendars, among others. Tap the switch to engage or disengage iCloud for this type of data.

3 Set up your computer and other devices to work with iCloud. For step-by-step instructions for each of your devices, go to www.apple.com/icloud/get-started/.

4 To review your data in the cloud, log in to www.icloud.com on a computer.

Install iTunes on your computer

On your iPad, the iTunes app connects you to the iTunes Store, where you purchase music, movies and so on, and you play back your purchased media, as it's called, using different iPad apps. But the iTunes application that runs on your computer handles purchases as well as playback, not to mention cable-based syncing. Moreover, movies and other rights-managed media that you buy on your iPad probably won't play on your computer in anything other than iTunes, so downloading the software is a wise choice. You'll also like the price. It's free.

1 On your computer, browse to www.apple.com/itunes.

2 Click the download button, and download the application into the folder of your choice.

3 Once the download is complete, browse to the folder where you saved the downloaded file. Double-click the file to start the installation.

4 Connect your iPad to your computer, and follow the onscreen instructions to register your iPad and set up an account with the iTunes Store.

? DID YOU KNOW?

You must log in to make purchases in iTunes, so make sure that your login information is easy to remember.

Sync using iTunes

When you *sync* or synchronise your iPad and your computer, you copy data, media and apps between them, so that they both have identical sets. Syncing enables you to enjoy your purchases across devices, and since the files reside in two places instead of just one, you insure yourself against lost or 'borrowed' iPads. The syncing process starts whenever you connect your iPad to your computer and launch your computer's iTunes application.

1 Plug the wider, flatter end of your iPad's cable into the iPad's dock connector.

2 Plug the thinner, longer end of the cable into a USB port on your computer.

3 If iTunes on your computer doesn't launch automatically, launch it manually.

4 Look for the sync icon to appear in the upper left corner of your iPad's display.

? DID YOU KNOW?

You can determine exactly which files to sync and when by clicking your iPad's name under Devices in iTunes on your computer.

WHAT DOES THIS MEAN?

Syncing: The process of copying data and applications from your iPad to your computer (and vice versa), so that both devices are current with the same data and apps.

5 Look for the sync icon to appear next to your iPad's name under Devices in iTunes on your computer.

6 To disconnect the iPad, click the eject button in iTunes, and then remove the cable from your computer. Don't remove the cable without clicking the eject button first.

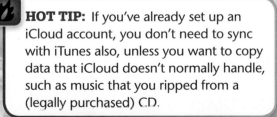

HOT TIP: If you've already set up an iCloud account, you don't need to sync with iTunes also, unless you want to copy data that iCloud doesn't normally handle, such as music that you ripped from a (legally purchased) CD.

Connect to the iPad Dock

The iPad Dock is an optional accessory that you might want to think about buying. It's a small, handsfree stand for your iPad for those times when you're relaxing at home (or relaxing at the office). Docking your iPad is especially useful when you're listening to music or doing something that doesn't require much interaction with the screen. As an added convenience, while your iPad is docked, you can charge its battery.

1 Connect your iPad to the iPad Dock by way of your iPad's dock connector.

2 Optionally, connect the cable to the back of the dock and then into a computer or an AC outlet to charge the iPad.

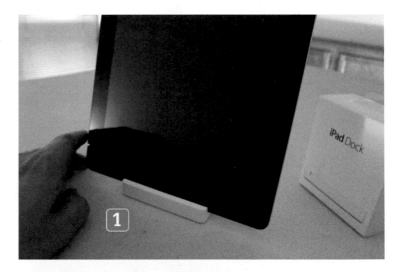

? DID YOU KNOW?
The iPad Dock also has a Line Out connection for attaching external speakers.

🔥 HOT TIP: When the iPad is sitting upright in the dock, you might find it uncomfortable to do much in the way of typing on the virtual keyboard. But if you accessorise your iPad with the Apple Wireless Keyboard, you can type as much as you like without disturbing the docked iPad.

Use wired headphones

Want to listen to something but need to keep the sound down? Consider using headphones. There is an external headphone jack on the top of the iPad.

1 Connect headphones to the iPad.

2 Listen to music, a movie, an audiobook or whatever you feel like listening to.

3 Control the volume using the volume switch on the side of the iPad.

? DID YOU KNOW?

When you have headphones plugged into your iPad, you can't hear sounds from your iPad's external speaker.

Connect a Bluetooth device

Bluetooth technology enables devices to communicate wirelessly. Typically, the devices need to be within a few metres of each other. To use Bluetooth on the iPad, you must first engage the Bluetooth feature and then pair a compatible Bluetooth device with the iPad. One popular option is the Apple Wireless Keyboard, which you can use in place of the virtual one, as shown below.

1 Place a Bluetooth device near the iPad, and turn the device on if necessary.

2 From the Home screen of the iPad, tap Settings.

3 Tap the General item in the Settings list.

4 On the list of general options that appears on the right, tap Bluetooth.

5 Engage Bluetooth by tapping the On/Off switch. Your iPad detects the Bluetooth device from step 1.

6 Tap the listing for this device to connect.

7 Use the device with your iPad.

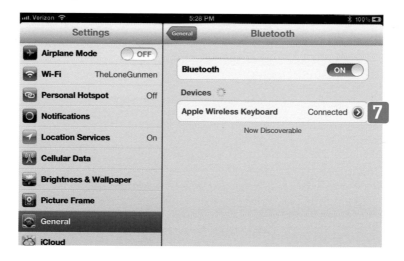

2 Setting up your iPad

Introduction

Chapter 1 provided an introduction to the most vital points that you need to know about your iPad – such as how to turn it on! In this chapter, you start to personalise your iPad and learn more about its features.

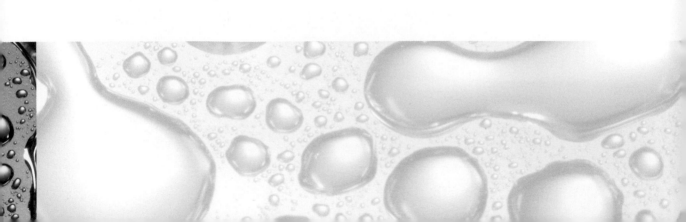

Set up an email account

Using your iPad for email is a no-brainer. You can even set up multiple email accounts.

1 In Settings, tap the Mail, Contacts, Calendars item.

2 In the list of options that appears, tap to add an account.

3 Select an email provider. You may already have an email account with one of these providers. If so, that's fine; you can simply enter your existing information.

4 Fill in the required information. You might need to go through a sequence of screens. When you're finished, tap the Save button.

5 Continue adding as many email accounts as you like.

? DID YOU KNOW?
If you use more than one email account, your iPad's Mail app can combine your inboxes so that you see all your emails from all your accounts in a single list.

Rearrange icons

The icons for all your core apps appear on the Home screen. As you download new apps, your iPad adds icons for them on additional views of the Home screen. You can see these extra rows of icons by swiping your finger across the screen in the direction that you want to push the current set of icons. (A small series of dots beneath the icons shows the number of views of the Home screen there are.) But if you would prefer a different system of organisation, you can rearrange the icons to suit your fancy.

1 Tap and hold your finger on any icon. All the icons begin to jiggle. Then hold your finger down on the icon that you wish to move; this doesn't have to be the one that you used to start the jiggle.

2 Drag the icon to another place on the screen. You can even drag the icon onto one of the other views of the screen by dragging it to the current screen's edge.

3 Remove your finger from the icon to drop the icon into place.

4 When you have finished rearranging icons, press the Home button to stop the icons from jiggling.

? DID YOU KNOW?

You can move but not delete the icons for the core apps, but you can delete the icons for any other apps. When the icons are jiggling, the icons for the non-core apps show a small X in the upper left corner. Tap this X to delete the icon and uninstall its associated app.

Change the wallpaper image

If you get tired of looking at the same old screens, you can change their background image or *wallpaper*. Use one of the iPad's built-in wallpaper images, or use a photo of your own; see Chapter 7 for how to work with photos.

1 In Settings, tap the Brightness & Wallpaper item.

2 In the list of options that appears, you see thumbnail images of the current Home screen and Locked screen. Tap either thumbnail.

3 To use a wallpaper image, tap Wallpaper, and choose an image from the list that appears.

4 To use a photo of your own, tap Camera Roll, and choose a photo from the list that appears. (Your Camera Roll collects all the photos on your iPad.)

5 Your iPad shows you a preview of the modified display. Tap the Set Lock Screen button, the Set Home Screen button or the Set Both button to use this image on the Lock screen, the Home screen or both screens; or tap Cancel to go back to Options.

HOT TIP: If you've set up the iCloud Photo Stream, or if you've created photo albums of your own, you can choose photos from these sets as well.

Search your iPad

Your iPad's search feature, called Spotlight, can look through everything on the iPad – all the email, notes, messages, media and data – and return a tidy, categorised list of results for whatever you might need to find.

1 Place a finger on the Home screen and swipe to the right. You might need to repeat this step a couple times, depending on which view you're currently seeing. You'll know you're in Spotlight when you see a search bar and the virtual keyboard.

2 Enter a search term in the field. As you type each letter, Spotlight filters the list of results automatically.

3 Tap a result to display it in the appropriate app.

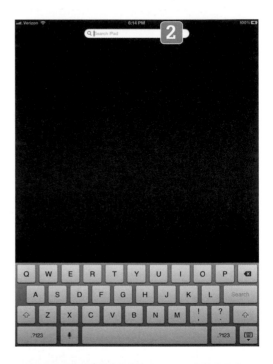

Secure your iPad with a passcode

Your iPad might contain sensitive data, and you might not always be around to protect it, so you can devise a four-digit passcode to keep your information confidential.

1 In Settings, tap the General item.

2 In the list of general settings, tap Passcode Lock.

3 Tap Turn Passcode On.

4 In the box that appears, enter and confirm your four-digit passcode. You can make the passcode whatever you like.

5 With the passcode enabled, you must enter the passcode whenever you attempt to use your iPad from the Off or Sleep state.

HOT TIP: To turn the passcode off, go back into Settings under General > Turn Passcode Off. You must enter the passcode one more time to disable it.

ALERT: A good passcode is one that is difficult for others to figure out. For example, don't use your birthday, but go ahead and use Mervyn Peake's (9 July 1911).

Back up your iPad

Backing up your iPad ensures that you don't lose any valuable data in the event that you must fix or replace your iPad.

1 If you use iCloud, you can automatically back up your iPad to the cloud whenever you connect the iPad to a power source, log into a WiFi network or lock the iPad. To engage the auto-backup feature, look under Settings > iCloud > Storage & Backup.

2 To restore your iPad from an iCloud backup, reset your iPad by tapping Settings > General > Reset > Reset All Settings, and then choose to restore your iPad from an iCloud backup during the setup process.

3 To back up your iPad with iTunes on your computer, connect the iPad to your computer and launch your computer's iTunes application.

4 To restore your iPad from an iTunes backup, connect the iPad to your computer, launch iTunes, and click Restore in the Summary tab.

DID YOU KNOW?

Simply by performing routine backups, you drastically reduce your risk of losing important data.

Maximise the charge in the battery

Out in the world, you can't always find a wall socket, so you want the charge in your iPad's battery to last. Here are some ways to slow down the drain.

1 Lower the brightness of the screen under Settings > Brightness & Wallpaper.

2 Turn off Cellular Data Service under Settings > Cellular Data.

3 Turn off Wi-Fi under Settings > Wi-Fi.

4 Turn off Bluetooth under Settings > General > Bluetooth.

5 Decrease the length of time before your iPad puts itself to sleep under Settings > General > Auto-Lock.

6 Turn off the iPad when you aren't using it for a significant length of time.

ALERT: Don't disable both cellular data and Wi-Fi if you need an Internet connection.

3 Shopping for music, movies and apps

Introduction

Your iPad does a lot right out of the box, but it does even more when you give it some media. From music and audiobooks to movies and TV shows, the iPad is designed to play it all. In some cases, you can transfer media files from a computer, but you can also purchase your favourite titles direct to your iPad from the iTunes Store. Likewise, you can purchase entirely new apps to expand your iPad's functionality. This chapter covers the ins and outs of browsing and buying from iTunes and the App Store.

Visit the iTunes Store

The iTunes Store is where you preview and purchase music, movies, TV shows, podcasts and audiobooks. There is a vast amount of media available in each format. You can filter the offerings by what is featured, by what is selling best (Top Charts) and by genre or category.

1 From the Home screen, tap the iTunes icon to connect to the store. You need to have an active Internet connection.

2 Have a look around the store to acquaint yourself with what you can find here.

3 At the top of the iTunes Store, tap Top Charts to see the best-selling media.

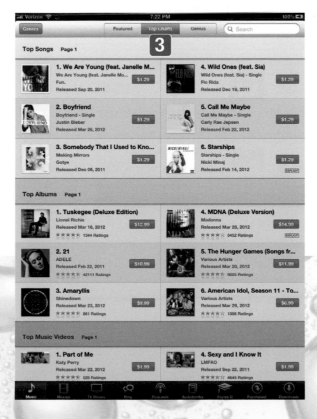

4 Alternatively, you can tap the Genres (or Category) button to filter the available selections. Tap the genre of your choice.

5 Choose from the selections that appear, or keep browsing.

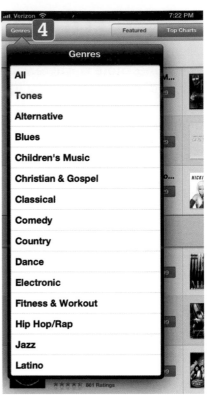

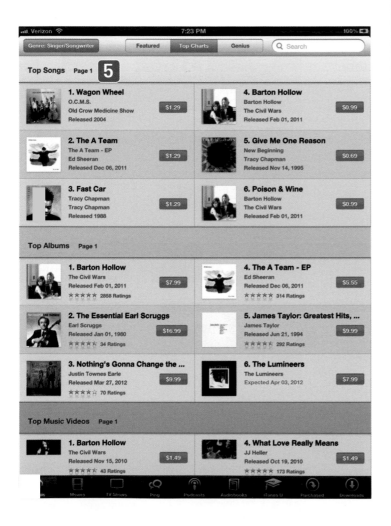

HOT TIP: Using the Featured, Top Charts and Genuis buttons, you can browse the store's selections.

Search the iTunes Store

When you know what you want, or to see whether an artist has a new release or whether a new movie is available for purchase, the search feature is just what you need.

1 Tap the search field in the upper right corner of the store interface, and enter the name of an artist, a title or a subject. The store presents suggestions to you as you type.

2 Tap the desired item in the search results.

3 Review the matches from the store's inventory.

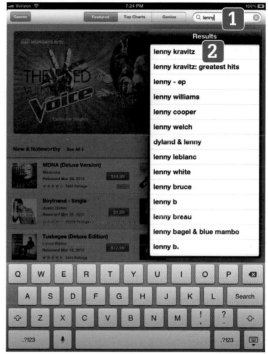

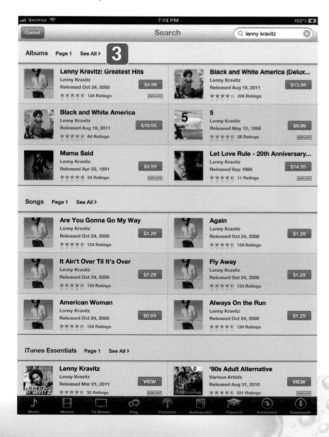

HOT TIP: To clear the search field, tap its X icon.

Preview media

In a brick-and-mortar store, you might pick up and look at an item before purchasing it. In the iTunes Store, you do the equivalent by previewing the item.

1 If you're looking at an album, tap a song to play a preview of that song.

2 If you're looking at a movie or TV show, tap to Preview to watch a trailer or short segment.

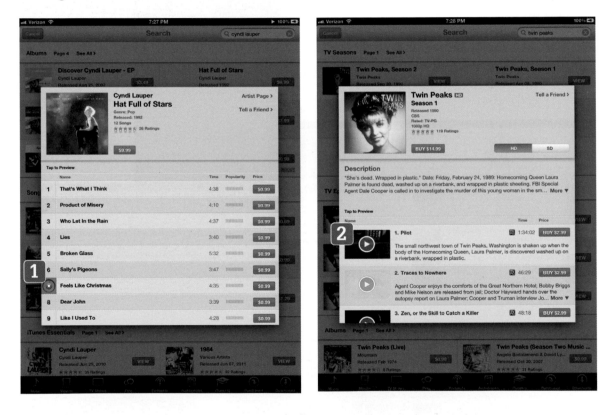

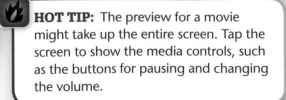

HOT TIP: The preview for a movie might take up the entire screen. Tap the screen to show the media controls, such as the buttons for pausing and changing the volume.

Purchase music

The iTunes Store enables you to buy entire albums or individual songs.

1 Find the item that you want to buy, and tap the price. If it's an individual song, tap the price for the song. If it's a full album, tap the price for the album.

2 The price changes to a confirmation message, such as Buy Song or Buy Album. Tap this button. If you aren't already logged in, the iTunes Store asks you to enter your Apple ID and password.

3 To prevent unauthorised purchases, the iTunes Store might ask for the password of your Apple ID. Type it in the field, and tap OK to start the download.

4 Once the download finishes, press the Home button, and then tap the Music icon to play your new music.

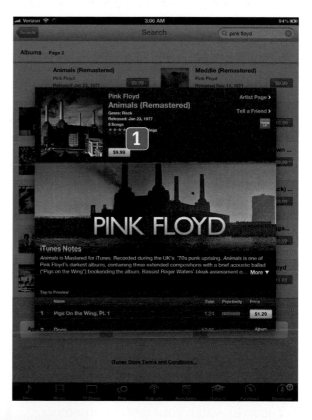

HOT TIP: You can review or change your payment method for Apple stores under Settings > Store > Apple ID. Tap View Apple ID, enter your password if necessary, and tap Payment Information.

HOT TIP: Make the Buy Album or Buy Song button revert to the price by tapping any empty space on screen.

Rent a movie

Quite a number of iTunes movies are available for rental. When you rent a movie from iTunes, your iPad downloads the movie, but it isn't yours to keep. Instead, you get it for a maximum of 30 days. Once you start watching it, you have 24 hours to finish. You can watch the movie as many times as you like over this 24-hour window, but afterwards, your rental is done, even if you watch it before your 30 days are over.

1 Find the movie that you want to rent, and tap the Rent button, which shows the price for the rental.

2 The price changes to the Rent Movie confirmation message. Tap this button. If you aren't already logged in, the iTunes Store asks you to enter your Apple ID and password.

3 To prevent unauthorised rentals, the iTunes Store might ask for the password of your Apple ID. Type it in the field, and tap OK to start the download.

4 Once the download finishes, press the Home button, and then tap the Videos icon to watch your rental. Remember, once you start watching it, you have 24 hours to finish, and don't wait longer than 30 days to start.

HOT TIP: You can rent some movies in high definition (HD) or standard definition (SD). Make sure to select the version that you want before you start tapping prices.

ALERT: When you rent a movie from your iPad, you must watch it on your iPad. You can't transfer the rental to another device the way you might with media that you purchase from iTunes.

Purchase a movie

If you'd rather own a movie outright, there's a good chance that you can purchase it from iTunes. Once you've purchased the movie, it's yours to keep, and you can transfer it to other devices for viewing.

1 Find the movie that you want to buy, and tap the price for purchase.

2 The price changes to the Buy Movie confirmation message. Tap this button. If you aren't already logged in, the iTunes Store asks you to enter your Apple ID and password.

3 To prevent unauthorised purchases, the iTunes Store might ask for the password of your Apple ID. Type it in the field, and tap OK to start the download.

4 Once the download finishes, press the Home button, and then tap the Videos icon to watch your movie.

? **DID YOU KNOW?**

Finding TV shows in iTunes is similar to finding movies, although you can buy individual shows or entire seasons (when available), and you can watch many shows free of charge. Go to the TV Shows section in iTunes to get started.

? **DID YOU KNOW?**

Standard definition looks fine on the iPad, but HD takes advantage of the iPad's high-density retina display for a truly spectacular experience.

🔥 **HOT TIP:** Just like with rentals, you can buy some movies in high definition (HD) or standard definition (SD). Make sure to select the version that you want.

Visit the App Store

The App Store is similar to the iTunes Store, only it sells apps. There are a bewildering number of apps to choose from in an equally staggering number of categories, and more are introduced as fast as developers can make them.

1 From the Home screen, tap the App Store icon to connect to the store. You need an active Internet connection.

2 The interface to the store fills the screen. Note the buttons along the bottom of the interface to help you browse the store: Featured, Genius, Top Charts, Categories, Purchased and Updates.

3 Under Featured, the top of the store's screen offers three ways to see what apps are available: New, What's Hot and Release Date. Tap the headings to sort the apps accordingly.

? DID YOU KNOW?

You can find newspapers and magazines in the App Store. From the Categories view, tap Newsstand, and take your pick. While many apps for periodicals are free, and while you often get some free content with each new edition that comes out, you usually need to buy a subscription to read the periodical from cover to cover. Launch your periodical apps from your iPad's Newsstand. Then, to place a subscription, look for a Subscribe button in the periodical's interface.

4 Using Categories at the bottom of the screen is a great way to browse through apps. Tap the Categories icon to see the assortment of categories.

5 Tap a category to see its apps.

6 View the apps in the selected category.

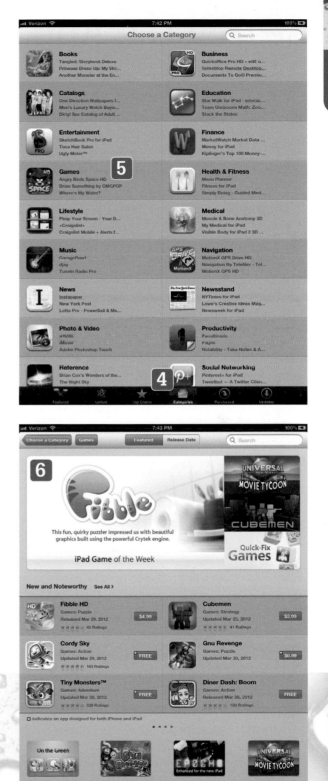

? DID YOU KNOW?

Some apps are free, while you pay to purchase others. But often an app that is free to download charges a price if you want to add extra features.

Search the App Store

You can search the App Store to find just what you need.

1 Find the search field in the upper right corner of the screen. Tap this field, and then enter the name of an app or the kind of app that you want to find. The App Store offers suggestions for you as you type.

2 Tap a search result.

3 Review the matches.

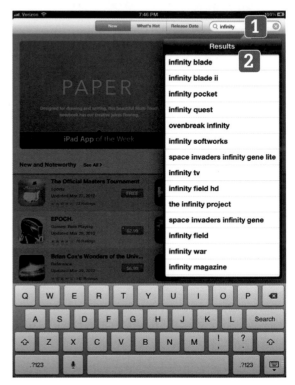

ALERT: The App Store might divide results into apps for the iPad and apps for the iPhone. Make sure that you focus on apps for the iPad. Apps designed for both display a small plus sign to the left of their price.

Purchase an app

You can download a free app without spending money, but for the ones that cost, you use the payment method associated with your Apple ID. Once you've downloaded the app, look for its icon on the Home screen, and then tap this icon to launch the app.

1 Tap the button with the app's price (or the button that says Free).

2 The price changes to the Buy App confirmation message. Tap this button. If you aren't already logged in, the iTunes Store asks you to enter your Apple ID and password.

3 To prevent unauthorised purchases, the App Store might ask for the password of your Apple ID. Type it in the field, and tap OK to start the download.

4 Watch the Home screen to monitor the progress of your new app's installation.

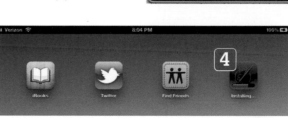

? DID YOU KNOW?

If video games are your thing, you might want to explore your iPad's Game Center app. The Game Center is a social network for gamers. Purchase a game from the App Store that's compatible with your iPad's Game Center, and you can track your achievements and worldwide high scores whenever you play with an active Internet connection. Even better, certain Game Center games enable you to challenge opponents from around the world! Who knows? You might even face me.

Delete an app

You can't delete your iPad's core apps, but you can delete any app that you download separately.

1 Tap and hold your finger on any icon. All the icons start to jiggle.

2 The icons of the apps that you can delete display a small X in the left corner. Tap the X to delete the app. (You don't have to delete the app whose icon you held down in Step 1.)

3 Tap Delete in the confirmation message that appears.

4 Press the Home button to stop the icons from jiggling.

> Delete "Pages"
>
> Deleting "Pages" will also delete all of its data.
>
> **3**
>
> Delete   Cancel

HOT TIP: You can delete as many apps as you like as long as the icons are jiggling. In fact, while the icons are jiggling, you can swipe the Home screen to see different sets of icons.

4 Surfing the Web with Safari

Introduction

The iPad is a great device for surfing the Web, and Safari, Apple's Web browser, is built right in. The iPad's version of Safari is a little different to the one that you might use on your computer. On older iPads, the differences were more pronounced, but the latest iPad brings the browsing experience even closer to what you get on a clunky old desktop or laptop computer.

Visit a website

Browsing the Web is just a tap away. Safari has a dedicated icon at the bottom of the Home screen.

1 Tap the Safari icon at the bottom of the Home screen. Your iPad launches the Safari app.

2 Find the address field at the top of the screen. Tap it to open the virtual keyboard.

3 Start typing in a Web address. Safari makes suggestions as you type based on the sites that you've already visited. Choose one of Safari's suggestions if you prefer.

4 Alternatively, type in the full Web address and then tap the Go key on the keyboard.

5 View the site.

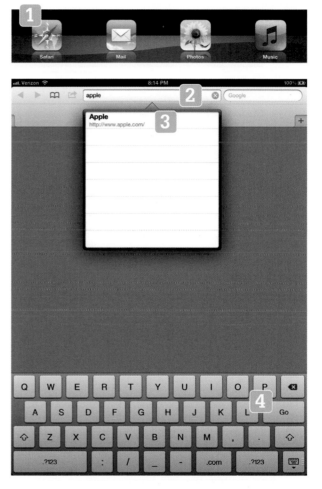

HOT TIP: When you launch Safari, you go back to the site that you last visited. If you don't want this to happen, make sure to close all open tabs before you return to the Home screen.

Search the Web

To the right of the address field is the search field. Enter a word or phrase to search the Web.

1 Tap the search field. The search field expands, and the virtual keyboard appears.

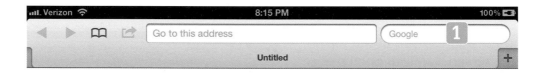

2 Start to type a search term. Safari offers suggestions as you go; you may tap any of these to finish, or you may keep typing.

3 Tap the Search key.

4 Review the results.

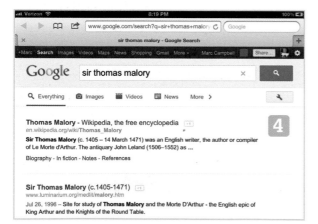

HOT TIP: Safari returns search results from Google by default. To use a different search service, look under Settings > Safari > Search Engine.

Create a Home icon to navigate directly to a website

When you launch Safari from the Safari icon, you start from the site that you visited last. But if you launch Safari from a custom Home icon, you begin directly in the site of your choosing.

1. In Safari, navigate to the desired website.

2. Tap the icon for options, which appears to the left of the address field. A menu appears.

3. Tap Add to Home Screen.

4. In the Add to Home box that opens, type a name for the icon, or use the name that Safari supplies by default.

5. Tap Add. Safari adds the icon for this site to your Home screen.

Open a new tab

If you're used to browsing on your computer, you probably know how to open tabs for viewing multiple sites at the same time. Each site appears in its own tab; to switch among the sites, you simply click the tabs. Owners of older iPads might remember how Safari didn't offer tabs and how you had to switch among sites with a confusing interface. But the latest iPad has corrected this inconvenience, so don't listen to anyone who tries to tell you that keeping current with your gadgets is merely an exercise in conspicuous consumption.

1 In Safari, find and tap the plus button. It's on the right side of the interface, just beneath the search field.

2 Safari creates a new tab and opens the keyboard. Type the address of the site to display in the new tab.

3 To switch among sites, tap their tabs.

4 Open as many tabs as you like by repeating these steps.

HOT TIP: Each tab has a small X on the left. Tap the X to close the tab.

Create a bookmark

If you find yourself visiting the same site over and over, why waste precious battery power typing and retyping the same address? Bookmarking a site for easy retrieval saves you from having to open the keyboard. You just tap the bookmark, and Safari loads the site.

1 When you are on a website that you wish to bookmark, tap the button for the options. It's immediately to the left of the address field.

2 Tap Add Bookmark. Safari opens the Add Bookmark box.

3 In the Add Bookmark box that appears, type the name for the bookmark, or use the name that Safari supplies by default.

4 If you want to add the bookmark to the Bookmarks Bar, tap the field at the bottom of the Add Bookmark box, and tap Bookmark Bar from the list that appears. Then tap Add Bookmark to go back to the Add Bookmark box.

5 Tap Save to create the bookmark.

? DID YOU KNOW?

The Bookmarks Bar is for the bookmarks that you use the most. For more information, see 'Use the Bookmarks Bar' next.

Use the History list

Need to find a site that you didn't bother to bookmark? Simply review your History list.

1 In Safari, tap the icon of the open book. If the list that appears doesn't say Bookmarks or History, tap the button in the upper left corner until you return to the Bookmarks list, and then tap History. Safari shows the History list.

2 The entries at the top of the History list are all the pages that you visited today. Tap an entry to navigate to the required page.

3 The entries for pages that you visited on previous days appear under their own folders. Tap a folder to see its list of pages, and then tap an entry to return to that page.

HOT TIP: To clear your History list, tap the Clear History button next to the title of the list, or look under Settings > Safari > Clear History.

Turn on Fraud Warning

The Internet is a network of people, and while most people are trustworthy, a few are not. *Phishing* is the practice of collecting confidential information from a form on a website somewhere. The site appears to belong to a known establishment, but in reality it's just a clever imitation, and the phishers are counting on you not to notice the difference. Using Safari's Fraud Warning feature helps you to avoid being duped.

1 In Settings, tap the item for Safari.

2 In the list of settings for Safari, find the option for Fraud Warning, and tap the On/Off switch to engage it.

ALERT: The Fraud Warning feature is not foolproof. If you visit a site that seems a bit shifty, trust your instincts and leave at once.

Block or allow pop-ups

Pop-ups are windows that open on top of the browser. You see them most often as advertisements. Although some good offers or information can occasionally pop up, most people find pop-up windows annoying and set their browsers to block them from appearing at all.

1 In Settings, tap the item for Safari.

2 In the list of settings for Safari, find the Block Pop-ups option. Tap the On/Off button to set the blocking feature on or off.

? DID YOU KNOW?

Not all pop-ups are advertisements. Some might deliver essential content or functionality. If a trusted site suggests browsing with pop-ups enabled, simply go back to Options and disable the pop-up blocker. You'll probably want to engage this feature again right before you leave the site.

Set how to accept cookies

Cookies are small files that your iPad downloads from a website, usually without your knowing about it. This might sound like a bad idea, but cookies are fairly standard on the Web, and they can't do anything active like a virus; they simply store the information that you have voluntarily provided, and they help to make your browsing experience richer or more personalised. You start running into problems when the advertisers on the site use their ads as a way to feed your iPad cookies of their own. These kinds of cookies help the advertiser to determine where you like to browse and what kinds of products and services you might be interested in buying. Blocking these cookies makes it just a little bit harder for overzealous marketers to target you online.

1. In Settings, tap the item for Safari.

2. Tap the Accept Cookies option.

3. In the Accept Cookies options, tap the From visited option, if it's not already selected.

4. Tap the Safari button at the top to return to Settings.

ALERT: The From Visited and Always cookie options might sound as if they are the same thing, but they aren't. Choosing the From Visited option prevents third-party advertisers from placing cookies on your iPad but accepts cookies from the site itself, while choosing Always accepts all cookies from all parties.

Browse in privacy

Safari offers a privacy setting. This feature blocks certain tracking techniques that online advertisers like to use to figure out how to sell you things. You can't prevent all unwanted snooping on the Web, but at least you can make advertisers work harder for it – and give them new reasons to drive up their prices.

1 In Settings, tap the item for Safari.

2 Tap the Private Browsing button to engage this feature.

3 Your iPad asks if you want to close your current tabs before engaging Private Browsing. If you don't close the tabs, your browsing won't be private on the sites in those tabs. Tap the Keep All button to keep the tabs open, or tap the Close All button to close them.

? DID YOU KNOW?

Privacy on the Web is a difficult issue, since by nature the Web is a public place. You should use your iPad however you like, but here's a rule of thumb, for what it's worth: Other people know which sites you're visiting, so stay away from the sites that you'd rather not be found in.

5 Staying in touch with Mail

Introduction

Can you email with the iPad? Of course you can! The email app on your iPad is called simply Mail, and it has a dedicated icon at the bottom of the Home screen. This chapter explains how to use Mail and how to tweak its options and features. If you need help setting up an email account, see Chapter 2.

Push or fetch

The title of this topic sounds like the punch line of an off-colour joke, but I promise you it isn't. *Push* and *fetch* describe two ways that an email server can deliver email to you. Under a Push scenario, the email server sends you email without your email app asking for it. You tend to get your email more quickly this way, but you use up more battery power, which isn't trivial for a mobile device like your iPad. Under Fetch, the email server doesn't send out your email until the email app specifically asks for it. You conserve battery power, but your email will have been sitting around for a while on the server before you receive it. You can configure Push and Fetch options for the Mail app in Settings.

1 In Settings, tap the Mail, Contacts, Calendars item.

2 In the list of settings that appears, tap Fetch New Data. A new list opens with options about Push and Fetch.

3 Tap the On/Off switch next to Push to enable the Push setting. You receive emails when they are sent, even when the Mail app isn't running, but you use more battery power.

4 Under Fetch, choose the duration for automatic email checks. The longer you wait, the less power you use, but the older your emails are when you finally get them. The setting that consumes the least battery power is Manually; but in this case, you get new email messages only when you check for them.

Settings	Fetch New Data
.ıl. Verizon 🛜	9:00 PM	100% 🔋

Settings

✈ Airplane Mode		OFF
🛜 Wi-Fi		TheLoneGunmen
🔗 Personal Hotspot		Off
⭕ Notifications		
🧭 Location Services		On
📡 Cellular Data		
☀ Brightness & Wallpaper		
🖼 Picture Frame		
⚙ General		
☁ iCloud		
✉ Mail, Contacts, Calendars		
🐦 Twitter		

Mail, Contacts... **Fetch New Data**

Push **3** **ON** 🟢

New data will be pushed to your iPad from the server.

Fetch

The schedule below is used when push is off or for applications which do not support push. For better battery life, fetch less frequently.

4

Every 15 Minutes	
Every 30 Minutes	
Hourly	
Manually	✓

Advanced	>

ALERT: Not every email service can push email. If yours doesn't, simply choose the shortest Fetch duration if you want to approximate a Push-like experience.

Read your email

The Mail icon sits at the bottom of the Home screen. If this icon displays a number, that's the number of unread emails waiting for you.

 1 Tap the Mail icon. Mail launches and checks for new emails to download.

2 Swipe to the right to open the list of messages in your Inbox.

3 Mail marks the emails that you have not yet opened with a blue circle. Tap an email to open it.

? DID YOU KNOW?

Just like the Safari app launches to show the last webpage that you visited, Mail launches to show the last mailbox that you viewed. If swiping in Step 2 gives you the contents of a different mailbox, tap the Mailboxes button at the top of the list, and then choose Inbox.

4 Read your email.

Inbox ▲ ▼   1 of 12

From: Billy Blind   Details

Front gatefold?
March 31, 2012 9:10 PM

4

Marl lookie here. Did you sign off on this? thx BB

billy blind | SPACE OPERA

🔥 **HOT TIP:** To check for new email at any time, tap the Refresh button at the bottom of the Mailboxes list.

Add a sender to your contacts

You can add the sender of any email to your contacts list, which makes it easier for you to contact this person in the future, whether by email or some other communication method.

1 Open an email, and tap the sender's name.

2 In the Sender box that opens, tap Create New Contact. Mail displays the New Contact box and fills in as much info about this person as the email provides.

3 Fill in any extra info if you wish, and tap the small Done button when you've finished. If the Sender box is still open, close it by tapping a blank area of the screen.

SEE ALSO: For more information about your contacts list and the Contacts app, see Chapter 12.

? DID YOU KNOW?

Now that you've added the sender as a contact, when you tap the sender's name in the future, the Sender box displays a number of different options, including Share Contact. Tap this button to share the sender's contact information with another person by email or instant message.

Compose an email

Mail enables you to compose email as well as receive it.

1 At the top of the Mail interface, tap the icon furthest to the right. Mail opens a blank email.

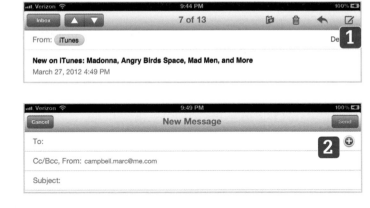

2 To the right of the To field, you see a plus sign (+). Tap it to display your contacts list, and then tap a contact's name to fill in his or her email address.

3 If you didn't use a contact in Step 2, type the recipient's email address in the To field.

4 Type the subject of the email in the Subject field.

5 Write your email.

6 When you've finished, tap the small Send button at the top of the email.

> **HOT TIP:** You can delete or change the signature line that appears by default at the bottom of your email. Look under Settings > Mail, Contacts, Calendars > Signature.

? DID YOU KNOW?

There's really no convenient way to attach a file to your email in Mail the way you can on a computer. But if you start in some other app – the Photos app for photos, for example – you can easily attach a file to an email when you choose to share the file. See the various Sharing topics in this book for step-by-step instructions.

Cut, copy and paste as you write

For your editing convenience, you can cut, copy and paste as you compose your email, but the procedure is a little different from that on a typical computer.

1. Tap and hold your finger on the text. A magnifying glass appears with a view of the text underneath. Drag your finger to position the cursor precisely where you need it.

2. When you release your finger, a bar appears with Select and other options. Tap Select. Your iPad selects the word to the right.

3. Tap and hold one of the small round handles that appear at the edges of the selection. Then drag the handle to make the selection smaller or larger.

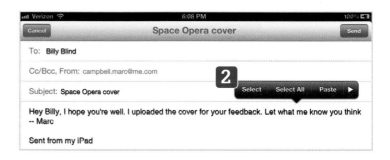

? DID YOU KNOW?
You can cut, copy and paste in many apps, not just Mail.

4 Tap a handle if necessary, and then tap Cut to copy and remove the text in the selection, or tap Copy to copy it without removing it.

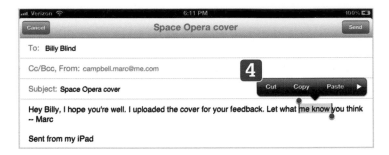

5 Tap elsewhere in the text.

6 Tap Paste. Your iPad inserts the copied text at the position of the cursor.

7 Check the results.

HOT TIP: The Cut Copy Paste bar also enables you to find definitions, replace the selected text and so on. The precise range of options depends on which app you're using.

Save a draft of an email

If you begin a new email but don't complete it straight away, you can save it as a draft and finish writing it later.

1 In the email window, tap the small Cancel button on the left. A choice appears to save or discard the email.

2 Save the email to move it to the Drafts mailbox.

Reply to an email

When you get an email and you want to reply, you don't need to compose a new email. Simply reply to the email that you received.

1 From the email to which you want to reply, tap the curved-arrow icon at the top of the interface.

2 From the menu that appears, tap Reply. Mail opens an email that contains all the text from the previous email or emails.

3 Compose your reply, and tap Send.

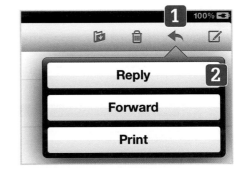

HOT TIP: When you receive an email sent to more than one person, you may choose Reply or Reply All in Step 2. Reply All sends the reply to everyone on the email.

Forward an email

Forwarding an email sends it to a new recipient without sending it back to the original sender.

1 From the email that you want to forward, tap the curved-arrow icon at the top of the interface.

2 From the menu that appears, tap Forward. A new email opens with the contents of the original email and an empty To field.

3 Type an email address in the To field, or tap the plus sign (+) to choose from your contacts list.

4 At the top of the email, type a brief greeting or explanation (if necessary), and then tap Send.

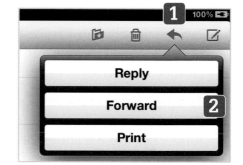

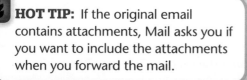

HOT TIP: If the original email contains attachments, Mail asks you if you want to include the attachments when you forward the mail.

Open an attachment

Sometimes your emails come with attachments of one type or another. Image and photo attachments appear in the body of the email, while other types appear as icons. You can open these kinds of attachments outside the Mail app.

1 Tap the attachment icon to open the attachment in your iPad's Quick Look app.

2 To open the attachment in a different app (perhaps with better support or more features for the attachment's file type), tap the icon for options in the upper right corner of Quick Look, and choose the name of an app from the menu that appears.

3 To return to the email, tap the Done button in the upper left corner of Quick Look.

! ALERT: If your iPad doesn't support an attachment type, you can see the attachment's name, but you can't open it. However, you might be able to purchase an app from the App Store that opens and reads computer files of this type.

🔥 HOT TIP: If the buttons overlay disappears in Quick Look, tap an empty area of the screen to bring it back.

? DID YOU KNOW?

For image and video attachments, you can save the image or video to your iPad's Camera Roll by holding down your finger on the attachment and choosing the Save command from the menu that appears. For more information about the Camera Roll, see Chapter 7.

Delete emails

Is your Inbox looking a little cluttered? Deleting some emails might be just what you need.

1. If necessary, open the email that you want to delete. Then, at the top of the Mail window, tap the Trash icon. Mail moves the email to the Trash mailbox but does not yet delete the email permanently. Stop here if that's good enough for you, or proceed to step 2 to clear out the Trash mailbox.

2. Switch to the Trash mailbox for your current email account, and tap Edit.

3. Tap the Delete All button near the bottom left of the screen.

HOT TIP: To pick and choose which emails to delete, open any mailbox, and tap its Edit button. Tap each email that you want to delete, and then tap Delete. Don't forget to go into the Trash mailbox afterwards to remove the emails from your iPad.

Search your email

You might not realise how useful Mail's search feature is until you've collected hundreds of emails from dozens of people over the course of a single weekend.

1 Switch to the mailbox that you want to search, and tap the search field at the top of the mailbox's email list. The virtual keyboard appears.

2 Type in the word or phrase to find. To limit the search to a particular field, tap From, To, or Subject. To search all three fields, tap All.

3 As you type, Mail displays matches. Tap a result to view the corresponding email.

4 To return to the mailbox's regular list, tap the Cancel button.

? DID YOU KNOW?

Don't forget that you can also use the Spotlight Search feature to search all your emails.

6 Socialising with Messages, FaceTime and Twitter

Introduction

Is email too old-school for you? Your iPad, social creature that it is, wants to keep you in touch with the people who matter, and it doesn't need to use email to do it. The lines of communication are open indeed, and this chapter shows you just a few of the options.

Text-chat with Messages

Your iPad's Messages app is for sending instant messages (or IMs) to your friends and family members. IMs are like the texts on your mobile phone, only you can attach images and other kinds of content to them. You can use the Messages app over Wi-Fi or your cellular data network, and you don't have to pay a per-message fee, but here's the catch: You can't just send your messages to any old mobile phone or chat program. Your chat partner needs to have an Apple device that runs the iOS5 operating system.

1 From the Home screen, tap the Messages icon. Your iPad launches the Messages app.

2 If necessary, open a new message by tapping the icon to the right of the Messages list (or tap an existing conversation from the list to pick up where you left off).

3 In the To field, type the telephone number or email address of your recipient, or click the plus button and choose from your contacts.

DID YOU KNOW?

When you use Messages over your mobile network, your texting rate doesn't apply. These messages go out over your cellular data service, not your texting service, but they *do* contribute to your monthly data limit.

4 Tap the message field just above the virtual keyboard, and type your message.

5 Tap Send to send your message.

6 Wait for the reply, and send another message back! The Messages app keeps track of the conversation.

HOT TIP: To attach a photo or some other media file to your message, tap the camera icon to the left of the message field.

Set notifications for instant messages

The Messages app notifies you by email when you receive an instant message while you're offline. The app can also notify your senders that you have read an instant message that they have sent to your Messages account.

1 From the Home screen, tap Settings.

2 From the Settings list, tap Messages.

3 Tap the Send Read Receipts On/Off switch to engage or disengage read receipts. With this setting engaged, the app notifies people who have sent you an instant message that you have read their message.

4 When you're offline, Messages sends your instant messages to your Receive At email address next to Receive At. To change this email address, tap it, and then tap Add Another Email and type the desired email address in the field that appears.

HOT TIP: Messages requires that you have at least one Receive At email address. If you have more than one, you can remove an address by tapping it and then tapping Remove This Email.

Make video calls with FaceTime

Text messages are great, but wouldn't you rather be chatting face to face? With the FaceTime app, you can do just that. FaceTime connects with any other FaceTime user over Wi-Fi. When you make a call, you get video and audio of your recipient, and they get video and audio of you. Of course, the devices on either end of the call need three things: the FaceTime app, a camera and a microphone. Your iPad has all three, as do newer iPhones and Mac computers.

1 From the Home screen, tap FaceTime. Your iPad launches the FaceTime app.

2 Tap the Contacts button at the lower right of the screen.

3 Choose a contact to call from the list that appears.

4 In the Info box that appears, tap the contact's mobile phone number or email address. FaceTime attempts to start a video call with this contact. If the connection succeeds, the call begins.

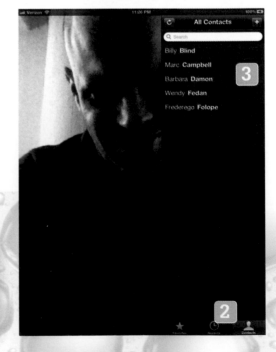

HOT TIP: You can also choose a person to call from your Favorites and Recents lists, which appear when you tap the Favorites and Recents buttons at the bottom of the screen.

5 To mute the audio from your microphone, tap the microphone icon. Tap the icon again to unmute the audio.

6 To switch from your iPad's front camera to the back camera, tap the camera icon.

7 To end the call, tap End.

Set up Twitter on your iPad

Twitter is a popular service for sharing the latest news from your world. Your updates or *tweets* are short text messages of 140 characters or less that go out over the Twitter network. People who follow your Twitter account receive your tweets immediately. The free Twitter app for your iPad enables you to send and receive tweets, and, if you don't already have a Twitter account, you can sign up for one without leaving the app.

1 From the Home screen, tap Settings.

2 Under Settings, tap Twitter.

3 To install the Twitter app, tap the Install button, and follow the onscreen instructions.

4 Once you have installed Twitter, tap its icon to launch the app.

5 If you already have a Twitter account, tap Sign In, and enter your Twitter login information.

6 If you don't yet have a Twitter account, tap Sign Up, and follow the onscreen instructions.

? DID YOU KNOW?

Once you've set up Twitter on your iPad, various other apps, including Photos, Maps and YouTube, can connect to your Twitter account for sharing. If you'd rather not share over Twitter from these apps, you can disengage the connections under Settings > Twitter.

HOT TIP: If you don't want to use the Twitter app, you can always log into your Twitter account over the Web in Safari. Browse to http://www.twitter.com.

Tweet from your iPad

Why should celebrities have all the fun? You can tweet just as well as they can, so get to it! Your followers receive your tweets immediately, but anyone with a Twitter account can find your tweets by searching. Remember, tweets are 140 characters or less, but you can attach images and other goodies to enhance their interest.

1 In the Twitter app, tap the composition icon at the bottom, on the left. A note page for your new tweet appears, along with the virtual keyboard.

2 Type the text of your tweet.

3 If you want to mention another Twitter user by name, precede his or her Twitter name with the at symbol (@), like this: @ iMarc3G. To see who's mentioned you in their tweets, look under Mentions in the Twitter app.

4 If you want to mark part of the tweet for search results, precede the search term with the hash tag (#), like this: #iPadTips. Now anyone who searches for the keyword iPadTips gets your tweet in the results.

5 If you want to attach a photo to your tweet, tap the camera icon, and choose the photo.

6 If you want to include your current location, tap the icon for Location Services. Tap this icon again, and choose Turn Off Location to remove your location information.

7 Tap Send.

> **HOT TIP:** To reply directly to another user's tweet, begin your tweet with the at symbol (@) and the user's Twitter name, like this: @iMarc3G ur iPad tips r gr8!

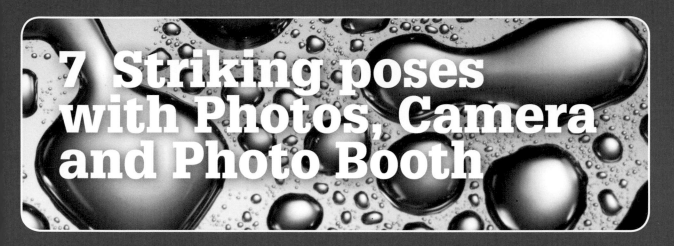

7 Striking poses with Photos, Camera and Photo Booth

Introduction

Photos and your iPad go together like they were destined to. From the viewing to the sharing and even the taking, your photos don't have a better friend this side of a digital camera. Several core apps are all about photos, and many of the others can work with photos, too. In this chapter, you learn all about the photo apps and get a sense of your iPad's photographic possibilities.

View photos

Photos is your iPad's app for viewing and organising your photo library. Notice the dedicated icon for this app at the bottom of the Home screen.

1 From the Home screen, tap the Photos icon. Your iPad launches the Photos app.

2 Find three buttons at the top of the Photos interface: Photos, Photo Stream and Albums. These buttons determine which photo thumbnails appear in the main viewing area of the app:

- Photos shows all the photos on your iPad.
- Photo Stream shows all the photos on iCloud. The photos that you haven't saved yet don't exist on your iPad, so they don't show up in any other view.
- Albums shows all the photos from a particular *album*, or collection of photos. Tap the album to see its photos.

3 To open a photo, tap its thumbnail.

4 Look at the photo that you opened.

5 Swipe the screen to move from photo to photo.

HOT TIP: To return to the current thumbnail view, tap the button in the upper right corner. The label on this button matches the name of the thumbnail view. If you don't see the button, tap once on the photo.

HOT TIP: Along the bottom of the screen is a small navigation bar. Move your finger across the bar to step through the photos in the current view. If you don't see the bar, tap once on the photo.

Create a photo album

The iPad stores all your photos in a sort of collection bin called the Camera Roll. Viewing the photos in your Camera Roll is great if you want to see everything you have, but it's not so great if you're looking for a particular group of photos. You can create these groups – or *albums,* as they're called – right from your iPad, and you can make as many of them as you like. You can move your photos from album to album, and you can even delete them from all your albums, without affecting the contents of your Camera Roll.

1 Start in Albums view. In Photos, tap the Albums button if necessary.

2 Tap the Edit button in the upper right corner. If you don't see this button, you probably need to back out of the current album into the view that shows all the albums on your iPad.

3 Tap the New Album button, which appears in the upper left corner.

? DID YOU KNOW?

Adding a photo to an album doesn't take the photo out of your Camera Roll; it just puts a 'pointer' from the photo in the Camera Roll to the album. So when you remove a photo from an album, your iPad simply erases the pointer, keeping the original photo safe and sound in your Camera Roll.

4 In the New Album box that opens, type the name of the new album, and tap Save.

5 Photos shows thumbnail images of all your photos. Tap the ones that you want to add to the new album, and then tap Done.

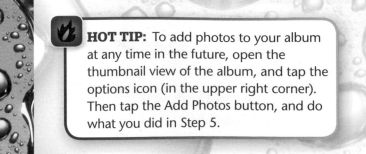

HOT TIP: To add photos to your album at any time in the future, open the thumbnail view of the album, and tap the options icon (in the upper right corner). Then tap the Add Photos button, and do what you did in Step 5.

Shrink or enlarge a photo

This is easy. Let your fingers do the work!

1 Open a photo.

2 Touch the screen with two fingers and move the fingers away from each other. The photo gets larger.

3 Use two fingers again. This time move the fingers towards each other. The photo gets smaller.

HOT TIP: You can enlarge a photo directly from any thumbnail view.

Run a slideshow

When tapping and browsing is just too much work, you can view any set of photos as a slideshow.

1 From any thumbnail view, tap the Slideshow button in the upper right of the screen. A list of options appears.

2 Select a *transition,* or the way that the slideshow changes from one photo to the next.

3 If you want to play music during the slideshow, tap to engage Music, and select from the music on your iPad.

4 Tap the Start Slideshow button.

HOT TIP: At any time while the slideshow is running, simply tap the screen to stop playback.

Use Picture Frame

When the iPad displays the Lock screen (the screen with the Slide to Unlock slider switch), you also see an icon for Picture Frame. Tapping this icon starts a slideshow.

1 In Settings, tap the Picture Frame item, and review the options that appear. These settings control how the slideshow displays your photos as well as which of your photos to use.

2 When the Lock screen is showing, tap the icon for Picture Frame, which looks like a flower. The slideshow begins.

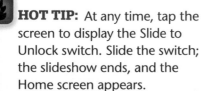

HOT TIP: At any time, tap the screen to display the Slide to Unlock switch. Slide the switch; the slideshow ends, and the Home screen appears.

Share a photo

Your iPad provides many different ways to share photos with your contacts.

1 With a photo displayed, tap the icon for the options in the upper right of the screen. This icon looks like an arrow inside a square. A list of options appears.

2 If you want to email the photo, tap Email Photo. Your iPad launches the Mail app, opens a new email, and embeds the photo in the body of the email. Type any additional text, address the email and send.

3 If you want to send the photo in an instant message, tap Message. Your iPad launches the Messages app and adds the photo as an attachment. Type any additional text, choose a contact and send.

4 If you want to tweet the photo, tap Tweet. Your iPad attaches the photo to a new tweet. Type any additional text, and send.

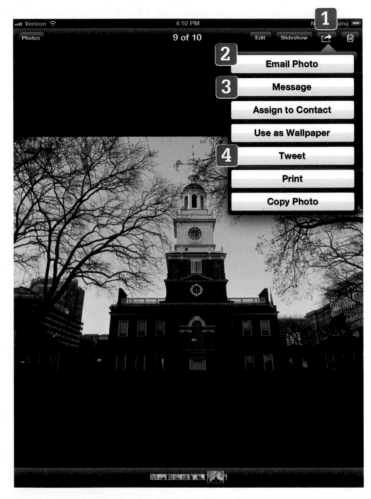

SEE ALSO: To tweet, you need a Twitter account. For more information about Twitter, see Chapter 6.

Take a photo with your iPad

For those times when someone tells you, 'Take a picture; it'll last longer,' your iPad comes with a built-in digital camera. The default lens is on the back, in the upper left corner (or the upper right corner when you're looking at the screen). You use the Camera app to take the photos, which go to your Camera Roll and, if you're on iCloud, they also go into your Photo Stream for distribution to all your iCloud devices.

1 From the Home screen, tap Camera. The Camera app launches.

2 Hold your iPad so that the lens on the back points towards your subject. The screen shows what the lens sees. To zoom in on your subject, use the pinch gesture.

3 Tap the round button with the camera icon on the right side of the screen to take a picture.

ALERT: The Camera app uses Location Services to determine your location. If you don't want to include location information in the photos that you take, make sure that you disengage Location Services for the Camera app under Settings > Location Services.

HOT TIP: If you want to take a picture with the lens on the front of your iPad – the one that you use for Photo Booth and FaceTime – tap the button with the camera icon and two curved arrows, which you find at the bottom of the screen towards the right.

? DID YOU KNOW?
You can use the Camera app to shoot video, too. In Camera, find the Camera/Video switch in the lower right corner, and tap it to alternate between still photos and videos.

Delete a photo

Deleting a photo is as easy as tapping the Trash icon – usually. The only time you really, truly delete a photo is when you delete it from the Camera Roll. When you delete a photo from one of your albums, you simply remove it from that particular album. The photo itself continues to exist quite happily in the Camera Roll.

1 Display the photo.

2 Tap the trashcan icon. A confirmation message appears, telling you exactly what will happen to the photo if you choose to delete it. This message changes depending on whether you're viewing the photo in an album or the Camera Roll and whether you've assigned the photo to an album.

3 Tap the Delete Photo button to proceed, or tap anywhere else to cancel.

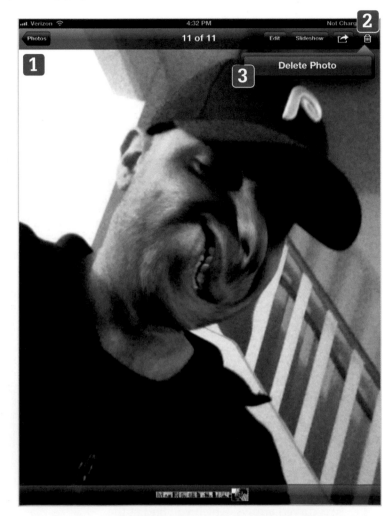

Import photos using the iPad Camera Connection Kit

The iPad Camera Connection Kit is an optional accessory that you can purchase for your iPad. With this kit, you can transfer photos to your iPad directly from your digital camera. The kit comes with two adaptors: one for SD camera memory cards and one for USB. If your camera doesn't use SD memory cards or doesn't have a USB connection, don't buy this kit.

1. Connect the USB adaptor from the Camera Connection Kit to the iPad. One side of the adaptor fits in the dock connector, and the other accepts a USB cable.

2. Run a USB cable between the camera and the connector, and turn the camera on. Skip ahead to Step 5.

3. If you don't have a USB connection on your camera, attach the SD adaptor from the Camera Connection Kit to the iPad. One side of the adaptor fits in the dock connector, and the other holds an SD memory card.

4. Remove your camera's SD memory card, and insert it in the adaptor.

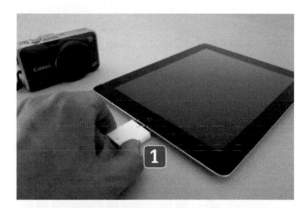

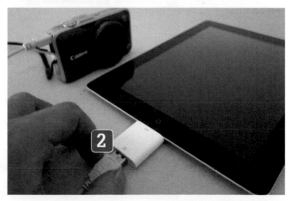

5 The iPad senses that there are photos from a new source: namely, the camera or the memory card. The screen shows these photos as thumbnails. Tap the photos that you want to import, or tap the Import All button to select them all.

6 Turn off your camera if it's connected to the iPad, and remove the adaptor.

8 Watching movies and videos

Introduction

Apple's marketing people like to boast that your iPad has a *retina display*. The idea is that the resolution of the screen is so high that the human retina can't distinguish the pixels. I don't know if I'd go that far, but the picture does look impressively crisp, and your video content – especially in high definition – is a feast for the eye, if not for the retina. The two apps for video are Videos and YouTube, and in this chapter, you explore them both.

Watch a movie in Videos

Whether you bought or rented a movie from iTunes, the chances are good that you want to watch it. As soon as it has finished downloading, it's ready to play in the Videos app.

1. On the Home screen, tap the Videos icon.

2. In Videos, tap the Rentals or the Movies button to see the movies that you have rented or bought.

3. Tap the movie that you want to watch.

4. From the information screen that opens, tap the Play button.

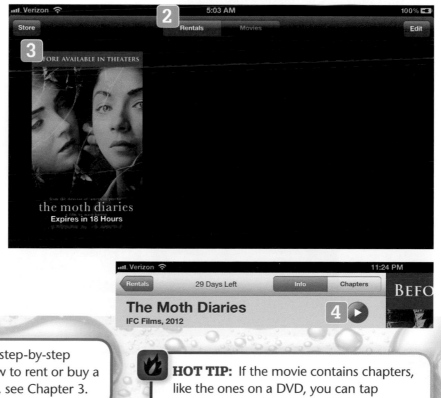

SEE ALSO: For step-by-step instructions on how to rent or buy a movie from iTunes, see Chapter 3.

HOT TIP: If the movie contains chapters, like the ones on a DVD, you can tap Chapters on the information screen to view the chapters in a list. Tap a chapter to start watching from that point.

Control video playback

Need to pause? Fast-forward? Rewind? Videos' playback controls are easy to use, but they stay out of the way until you need them.

1 While the movie is playing, tap the screen. Videos displays an overlay with the playback controls.

2 To jump to the previous chapter, tap the Back button.

3 To pause the movie, press the Pause button; press this button again to resume playback.

4 To jump to the next chapter, tap the Forward button.

5 To change the volume, drag the slider beneath the playback controls.

6 To fast-forward or rewind the movie, drag the slider along the top of the screen.

7 To return to the movie's information screen, tap Done.

HOT TIP: If the movie doesn't fill the entire screen, you can zoom in by tapping the button to the right of the top slider, although you'll also lose the extreme left and right sides of the movie frame. To return to the original zoom level, tap this button again.

Delete a movie

You paid for it. You watched it. You hated it. Delete it.

1 Hold your finger on the movie until a small X appears.

2 Tap the X.

3 Videos asks you if you want to delete the movie. Tap Delete and be done with it.

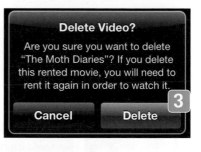

? DID YOU KNOW?

Movie rentals automatically delete themselves 24 hours after you first start watching them. If you never start watching them, they delete themselves after 30 days.

Watch a YouTube video

YouTube is a website of millions of user-generated videos. They're usually short and often silly, and they make for good momentary diversions from the bustle of your day. You can visit YouTube in Safari on your iPad by going to m.youtube.com, or you can use your iPad's built-in YouTube app, as you do in this task.

1 On the Home screen, tap the YouTube icon.

2 Tap the categories at the bottom of the YouTube app to see various video selections, including Featured, Top Rated and Most Viewed.

3 When you find a video you like, simply tap it to start playback.

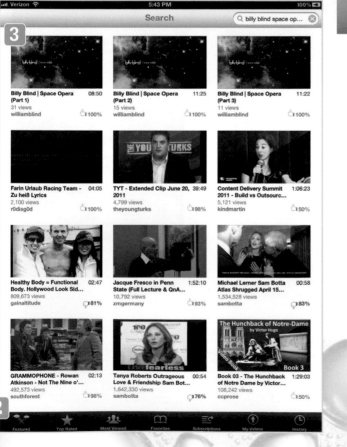

? **DID YOU KNOW?**
A video's rating comes from the average of all user ratings.

4 While the video is playing, tap it to reveal the playback controls and other YouTube features.

5 To exit the video, tap the button at the upper left of the screen.

HOT TIP: To view the video in full-screen mode, tap the double-arrow icon to the right of the playback slider. (You might need to tap the video to see this control.) Tap the double-arrow icon again to return to the regular interface.

Search for a YouTube video

Don't know where to start? Search for your favourite performer, passion, pastime or comical situation, and see what kind of videos YouTube has for you.

1 In the YouTube app, tap the search field at the upper right of the screen, and type in what you'd like to find.

2 Tap the Search key on the virtual keyboard. YouTube displays a page of results.

3 Tap a movie in the results to start watching.

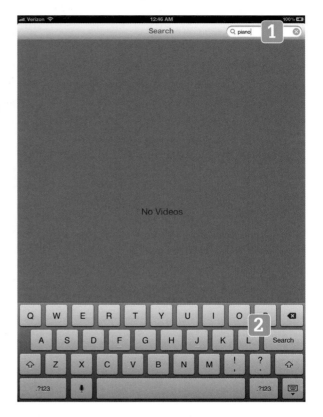

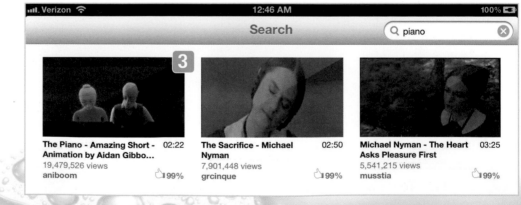

HOT TIP: Search for a more specific term to get more focused results.

DID YOU KNOW?
Don't forget to scroll the page. There are probably more results hiding below the bottom of the screen.

Connect your iPad to a television

Depending on the connections on your television, you can buy an adapter kit from Apple that turns your TV into an iPad display. You can watch movies, look at photos, surf the Web, and so on, all from your TV screen – at least in theory. Some users claim that the adapter doesn't always work with certain movies or apps, so 'your mileage may vary,' as the saying goes. There are two connector kits on the market: the Apple Digital AV Adapter for HDMI connections (on HDTVs) and the Apple VGA Adapter for VGA connections (on some TVs and computer monitors).

1. Connect the adapter cable to the dock connector of your iPad.

2. If you're using the Apple Digital AV Adapter, attach one end of an HDMI cable into the connector on your TV, and attach the other end of the cable into the HDMI connector on the adapter. If you're using the Apple VGA Adapter, do the same thing, only make it a VGA cable, and plug one end into your TV's VGA connector.

3 If you're using the Apple Digital AV Adapter, you can plug your iPad's cable into the dock connector on the adapter and then plug the other end of the cable into a wall socket. This way, you can charge the iPad's battery while you watch. The Apple VGA Adapter doesn't have a separate dock connection.

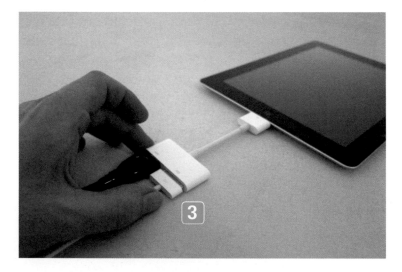

4 On the iPad, start a movie. The video should appear on your TV.

? DID YOU KNOW?
If you have a Wi-Fi network set up at home, you can purchase the Apple TV accessory, connect it to your HDTV, and stream video from your iPad wirelessly – no connection kit required.

! ALERT: The HDMI or VGA cable that runs between the TV and the adapter does not come with the Apple connection kit; you must buy this cable separately.

🔥 HOT TIP: Make sure you change the TV source to your HDMI or VGA input, depending on whether you're using the HDMI or VGA adapter.

9 Sound advice: Using the Music app

Introduction

Your iPad's app for playing audio was once called iPod, but now it goes by the name of Music. And while you probably plan to listen to a fair amount of music on your iPad, you can also use the Music app with audio podcasts and audiobooks. In this chapter, you learn how to organise your audio collection, find something to play, and play it.

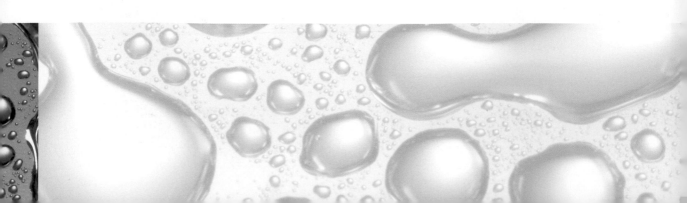

Browse your music library

This task assumes that you already have a music library on your iPad. If you don't, you can transfer the one from iTunes on your computer by syncing (see Chapter 1). And of course Apple would prefer it if you just went ahead and bought a brand new music library for your iPad from the iTunes Store (see Chapter 3). However you end up assembling your music library, you browse it like this.

1 Tap the dedicated Music icon at the bottom of the home screen.

2 Tap the buttons at the bottom of the Music interface to sort your library by album, artist, song, and so on.

3 Tap a letter in the list that appears down the right side of the screen to jump to the items in the current category view that begin with this letter.

HOT TIP: By default, Music sorts your music alphabetically by title. To sort alphabetically by artist instead, tap the More button, and then tap to engage the Sort By Artist On/Off switch.

4 Tap the Playlists button to show *playlists,* or collections of songs. You can create your own playlists from the songs in your library to make 'mix tapes'.

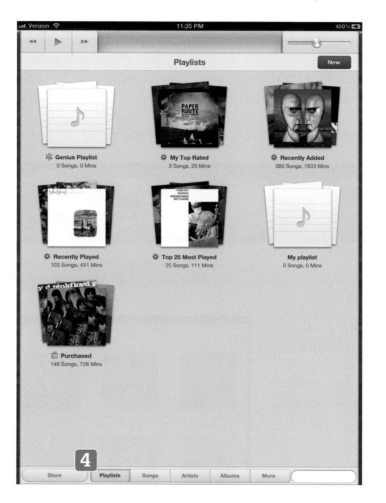

Listen to an album, song or playlist

Or an audiobook. Or a podcast. Whatever your category view in Music happens to be, you're just a tap or two away from audio.

1 From your library in Music, open your artists, albums or playlists until you find the audio file that you want to hear, and then tap this file. Music begins playing it.

2 To go back to the previous song in the album, the previous chapter in the audiobook, the previous item in the playlist, and so on, tap the Back button.

3 To pause playback, tap the Pause button; resume playback by tapping this button again.

4 To skip ahead to the next item, tap the Forward button.

5 To repeat all the songs in the current album or list, tap the repeat icon. To repeat the current song, tap this icon again. To resume normal playback, tap the icon again.

6 To fast-forward or reverse the current item, drag the red pointer along its playback slider.

7 To shuffle the current album or list, tap the shuffle icon. To resume normal playback, tap this icon again.

8 To change the volume, drag the volume slider at the top right of the screen.

HOT TIP: You can also increase or decrease the volume by clicking the volume buttons on the side of your iPad. To mute the audio entirely, hold down the button that lowers the volume.

View the Now Playing screen

The Music interface is nice enough, but the Now Playing screen is even better. This screen shows a nice, big version of the artwork for your audio, and it hides the playback controls until you need them. If you're just settling down with your favourite album or audiobook, give the Now Playing screen a try.

1 While an item is playing in Music, tap its cover art next to the playback controls. Music launches the Now Playing screen.

2 To show the playback controls, tap the screen. These controls work just like ones in the usual Music interface.

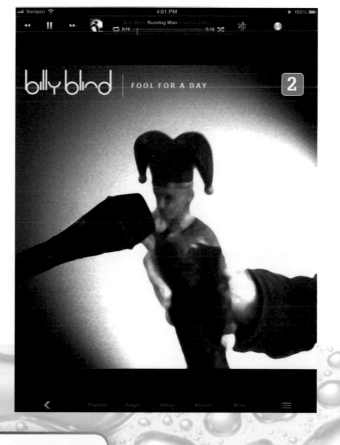

🔥 **HOT TIP:** Tap the screen again to hide the playback controls.

3 To switch between the cover art and the list of tracks, tap the list icon in the lower right corner of the screen. You can jump to a track by tapping it. Tap this icon again to revert to the cover art.

4 To return to the library view, tap the arrow icon in the lower left corner of the screen.

◁)	Running Man	Billy Blind	3:32
2	There's a Way	Billy Blind	4:16
3	How to Write a Hit Song	Billy Blind	3:08
4	D.O.A.	Billy Blind	5:38
5	Fly On (Yesterday's Gone)	Billy Blind	4:37
6	After the War	Billy Blind	6:05
7	We Phoenix	Billy Blind	3:58
8	Still No Wiser	Billy Blind	4:36
9	The Gate of Insanity	Billy Blind	3:37
10	Conservative Woman	Billy Blind	4:44
11	Come to You	Billy Blind	5:43
12	The Fantastic Freedom Institute	Billy Blind	3:35
13	Dangerous Days	Billy Blind	5:09
14	Heaven's Window	Billy Blind	3:16

Playlists   Songs   Artists   Albums   More

Create a playlist

A *playlist* is just a list of songs. Music plays them in order like the tracks of an album. There are a few automatic or *smart* playlists, including Purchased, Recently Played and Recently Added, that Music compiles on your behalf, but you can create your own playlists, too.

1 In Music, switch to the Playlists category of your library by clicking the Playlists button.

2 Tap New.

3 In the New Playlist box that opens, type the name for your playlist, and tap Save.

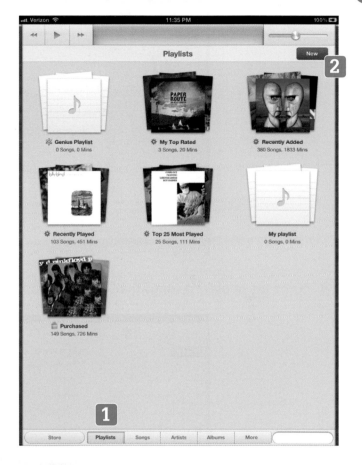

🔥 **HOT TIP:** You can browse to different category views while creating your playlist, as I did here.

4 Go through your music library, and tap the button with the plus sign (+) next to each song that you want to add.

5 When you're finished, tap Done.

6 In the list of playlist songs that appears, tap Done.

? DID YOU KNOW?

A song can appear in more than one playlist, and the same song can appear more than once in the same playlist.

Edit a playlist

You can change the song selection in your playlists whenever the mood strikes.

1 Open a playlist from the Playlists category of your music library, and tap the Edit button.

2 To add songs to the playlist, tap Add Songs, and then choose the songs to add from your music library. Tap Done to return to the playlist that you're editing.

3 To remove a song from the playlist, tap the red button to the left of the song name, and then tap the Delete button that appears.

4 To change the position of a song in the playlist, hold your finger down on the icon to the right of the song, and then drag the song to wherever you want to place it.

5 When you're finished editing the playlist, tap Done.

ALERT: Music doesn't display a confirmation message when you remove a song from a playlist, since your iPad doesn't delete the song from your library. If you make a mistake, simply add the song again.

Search your music library

As your music library grows, you'll find Music's search feature increasingly more useful.

1 In Music's library view, tap the search field in the lower right corner.

2 Enter a search term into the field. Music displays all the matches from the current category view.

3 To see all the matches from a different category view, tap the category that you want to see.

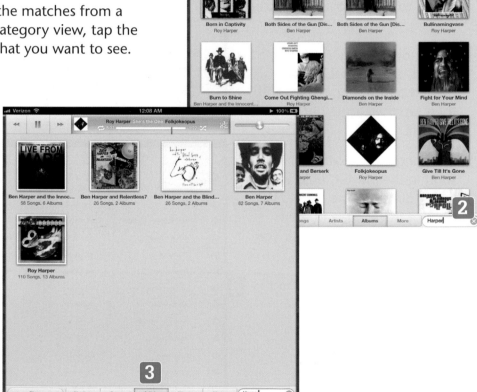

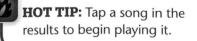

HOT TIP: Tap a song in the results to begin playing it.

Rate a song

Rating individual songs might be a little easier to do in iTunes on your computer, but you can also rate songs in Music on your iPad.

1 In Music, start playing a song, and switch to Now Playing view.

2 Tap the icon in the lower right of the screen to reveal the album's track list.

3 Swipe your finger along the row of dots above the track list. The dots become stars. You can rate the song from one to five stars, with five being the best.

> **HOT TIP:** Four- and five-star songs appear in the My Top Rated playlist.

> **? DID YOU KNOW?**
> You can change your rating for a song by repeating the steps in this task.

Listen to music while using another app

One of the great things about the Music app is that it doesn't need to appear onscreen in order for you to listen to audio. In fact, if you exit Music while audio is playing, the audio continues to play no matter what you're doing on your iPad, unless you need sound for some other feature (like playing a movie). You can even pause playback and skip or repeat audio selections without going back into Music.

1 Launch the Music app, and get some music playing.

🔥 **HOT TIP:** Cue up a lengthy playlist or an album, or enable the Repeat feature in Music. This way, you don't need to keep switching back to the Music app when the music stops playing.

2 Press the Home button. The Music app closes, but the music keeps playing. You're free to use your iPad however you like. To get back into Music, tap its icon.

3 To show playback controls from any app, press the Home button twice in quick succession. A bar of recent apps appears along the bottom of the screen.

4 Flick this bar to the right to see the playback controls. Use them, and then press the Home button again to hide them.

Delete audio from your iPad

While you can delete movies directly in the Movies app, the Music app doesn't give you a delete option for your audio files. You can still delete audio items from your iPad, but to do it, you need to go through iTunes on your computer.

1 In iTunes on your computer, select the audio to delete.

2 Choose Edit > Delete from the main menu.

HOT TIP: To restore audio files that you delete, you must first restore them to iTunes on your computer and then resync your iPad. This is why it's smart to keep the audio file after you delete it from your music library.

3 iTunes asks if you want to keep or delete the selected audio. Unless you need to free up some storage space on your computer, keep it.

4 Sync your iPad to iTunes. For step-by-step instructions, see Chapter 1.

Configure Music settings

If you listen to music frequently on your iPad, some of the options for the Music app might be of interest to you.

1 In Settings, click the Music item.

2 If some songs in your music library sound much quieter than others, you might want to engage the Sound Check feature. Sound Check applies *normalisation* to your audio files, which helps to reduce the difference in loudness among individual songs. To engage Sound Check, tap its On/Off switch.

3 If you enjoy a thudding bass response or prominent vocals, or if you tend to listen to a particular kind of music, you might want to adjust the equalisation. *Equalisation* helps to shape the tonal range of music by boosting or dropping certain frequencies. To choose an equalisation setting, tap EQ, and choose an equalisation profile from the list that appears.

4 To set a hard limit to the volume of the audio, no matter how much you turn up your iPad's volume, tap the Volume Limit option, and then set the maximum volume on the slider that appears. To disengage the Volume Limit feature, drag the slider all the way to the right.

? DID YOU KNOW?

If you want to prevent someone from overriding your maximum volume setting (such as a teenager who likes very loud music), tap the Lock Volume Limit button under Settings > Music > Volume Limit. Then, in the box that appears, enter and confirm a four-digit code of your choosing. Now, when the iPad's user tries to change the volume limit in Settings, this person must first supply the four-digit code.

HOT TIP: If you aren't sure which EQ setting to use, start playing a song in Music, and then come back to the EQ settings and go through the choices one at a time. Your iPad changes the sound of the audio immediately. When you find a setting that sounds good to you, keep it.

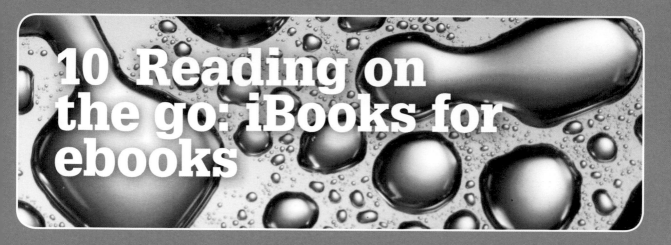

10 Reading on the go: iBooks for ebooks

Introduction

Electronic book readers have been around for years but with a lukewarm reception – until recently. The success of the Amazon Kindle and so on has rocketed ebooks to new heights of popularity. But even if you're not the sort to follow trends, you have to admit: e-reading is convenient and good for the environment. You can pack a lifetime of reading into a portable device and save the shelves in your flat for your most treasured volumes. Your iPad can download and read ebooks, too, but first you need the free iBooks app.

Install the iBooks app

The iBooks app doesn't come with your iPad, but you can download it from the App Store free of charge.

1 From the Home screen, tap the App Store icon.

2 Tap the search field, and search for *iBooks.*

3 In the results list, tap the app with this precise name.

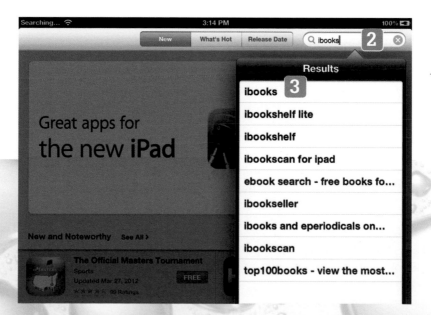

4 Tap the Install button to download and install the iBooks app. (You might need to supply the password for your Apple ID to proceed.) Your iPad adds an icon for it on the Home screen.

? **DID YOU KNOW?**

When you visit the App Store, your iPad might come right out and ask you if you want the free iBooks app. Go ahead and take the offer!

▶ **SEE ALSO:** See Chapter 3 for help with downloading and installing apps.

Browse the iBookstore

When you launch the iBooks app, you see your library of ebooks. But if you haven't downloaded any yet, your ebook shelf might be rather empty. The solution is clear: simply get some ebooks from the iBookstore. While you'll need to purchase the latest bestsellers, many of the greatest books ever written are yours free of charge.

1 From the Home screen, tap the iBooks icon. The iBooks app launches.

2 Tap the Store button in the upper left corner, and the iBookstore opens. The store interface resembles iTunes or the App Store, but here you find ebooks only (unless some special promotion is happening). If you want to buy audiobooks, shop at iTunes. If you want to subscribe to a periodical, try the App Store or the Newsstand.

3 The bottom of the iBooks app displays a row of buttons. Tap these buttons to view the different sections of the store.

4 Tap the Categories button at the bottom of the interface to sort ebooks by category, and then tap the category that you want to peruse.

HOT TIP: For a quick list of the most popular free ebooks, switch to Top Charts, and look under the Top Free Ebooks heading.

Search for an ebook

If you need to find a particular ebook or a particular author, try the iBooks search feature.

1 On the right side of the screen, tap the search field, and enter a search term. iBooks displays a list of matches as you go.

2 Tap a match.

3 Review the results in the iBookstore.

HOT TIP: To clear the search field, tap its X icon.

Sample an ebook before you buy

For many ebooks in the iBookstore, you can download a sample to read before you commit to the full purchase.

1 From anywhere in the iBookstore, tap an ebook. A box opens with details, ratings and comments about the ebook that you selected.

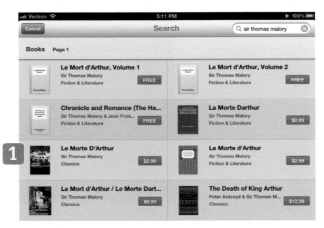

2 Just below the price of the ebook, you probably see a Get Sample button (although not all books offer samples). Tap Get Sample to place a preview of the ebook in your library.

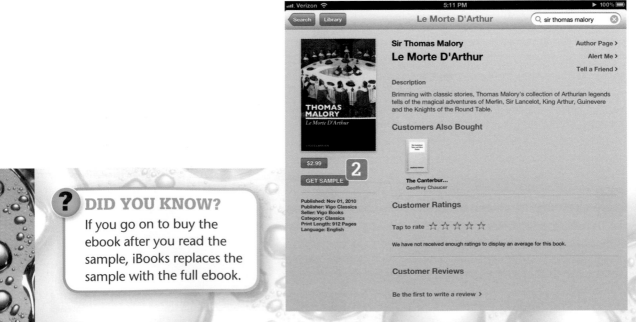

? **DID YOU KNOW?**

If you go on to buy the ebook after you read the sample, iBooks replaces the sample with the full ebook.

Purchase an ebook

The main purpose of the iBookstore is to sell you ebooks, so don't be surprised if you find something that you want to read. But remember, you can also find free editions of many of the classics. They're priceless in every sense of the word.

1 Find the ebook that you want to download, and tap on the price (even if it's free).

2 The price changes to the Get Book confirmation message. Tap this button. If you aren't already logged in, the iBookstore asks you to enter your Apple ID and password.

3 To prevent unauthorised purchases, the iTunes Store might ask for the password of your Apple ID. Type it in the field, and tap OK to start the download.

4 Once the download finishes, you find your new ebook on the shelf in iBook's Library view.

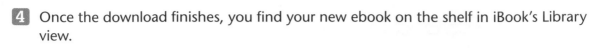

HOT TIP: You can review or change your payment method for Apple stores under Settings > Store > Apple ID. Tap View Apple ID, enter your password if necessary, and tap Payment Information.

DID YOU KNOW? You can redeem an iTunes gift card for purchases at the iBookstore.

View your library

Unlike the situation of Hansel and Gretel, no matter how deeply you wander into the 'forest' of the iBookstore, your 'home' (or ebook library) is just a tap away. No breadcrumbs required.

1 From the iBookstore, tap the Library button at the top of the interface.

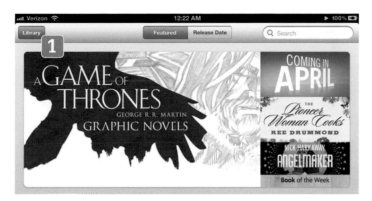

2 To switch to Bookshelf view, tap the first icon in the icon pair on the right. In Bookshelf view, you can switch to another shelf by swiping to the left or right. It might take a second or two for the shelf to change.

HOT TIP: In Bookshelf view, if you have more ebooks than room on your shelf, iBooks adds a new row to your shelf. Scroll up or down to move through you shelves.

3 To switch to List view, tap the second icon in the icon pair on the right. In List view, you can sort your library according to the order in Bookshelf view or by title, author or category by tapping the buttons at the bottom of the interface.

4 Whether you're in Bookshelf view or List view, there's a search field just above the uppermost shelf or the top list item. Scroll the shelf or list to reveal it, and then tap inside it and type a search term. As you type, iBooks filters the view so that you see ebooks with matching titles or authors.

Add bookshelves to your library

As you acquire more and more ebooks, you might want to organise them into bookshelves or *collections.* Each collection has its own shelf; swipe left or right to browse your shelves.

 1 In Library view of iBooks, tap the Collections button.

2 In the list of collections that appears, tap New.

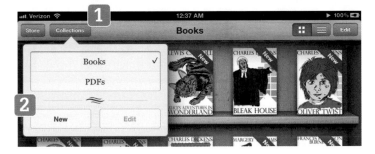

3 Type a name for the collection. When you tap Done, iBooks adds this shelf to your library.

4 From the list of collections, tap Books. iBooks closes the list.

5 Tap the Edit button.

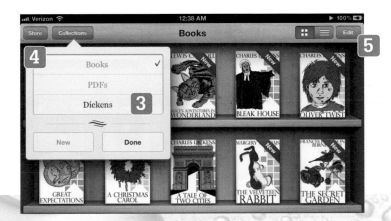

 **❓ DID YOU KNOW?**

You can move your ebooks around the shelves! Hold your finger on the ebook that you want to move. After a moment, the ebook becomes a little larger. Then just drag the ebook to where you want to move it, and release.

6 Tap the ebooks that you want to move to the new collection.

7 Tap the Move button. The list of collections appears.

8 Tap the collection that you created in Step 2.

9 Find your books on your new shelf.

HOT TIP: To delete a collection, tap Collections, and then tap the Edit button at the bottom of the list of collections. Tap the red circle next to any collection that you want to remove, and then tap its Delete button. If you have ebooks on a deleted shelf, iBooks asks whether you want to delete or move them; if you move them, they go back to their original shelves. Tap Done to exit Edit mode.

Open and read an ebook

As if downloading ebooks and organising your bookshelves were not excitement enough, iBooks also enables you to open and read your ebooks.

1 Tap the ebook that you want to read. The ebook opens to the first page (for a new download) or from where you left off.

2 To page forward or backward through the ebook, swipe to the left or the right.

3 To jump to a particular page, drag the page finder at the bottom of the interface.

4 To view the table of contents for the ebook, tap the button with the list icon, which appears to the right of the Library button. From the table of contents, tap the Resume button to go back to your previous page.

5 To return to your library, tap the Library button.

ALERT: Not all books have a table of contents.

HOT TIP: To make the controls disappear while you read, tap any blank space on the page. Tap again to make the controls reappear.

Set the brightness of the pages

A bright ebook in a dark room or a toned-down ebook in sunlight? We all have our preferences for how bright the screen should be. It's easy to change the screen's brightness for reading.

1 From any page of the ebook, tap the first button in the upper right corner, the one that looks like a pair of As. A menu of options appears, along with a slider control.

2 Drag your finger along the slider to change the brightness of the screen.

When you change the brightness setting in iBooks, you affect the brightness setting for your iPad on the whole. Similarly, when you adjust the brightness setting under Options, you change the brightness setting in iBooks, too.

Set the type size, typeface and paper style

To make for more comfortable or enjoyable reading, you may alter the size of the type as well as the typeface and even the look of the digital paper.

1 From any page of the ebook, tap the first button in the upper right corner. This button looks like a pair of As.

2 In the list of options that appears, tap the button with the larger letter A to increase the type size, or tap the button with the smaller A to decrease the type size.

3 Tap the Fonts button to see a selection of fonts, and then choose a font for the ebook's typeface.

4 Tap the Theme button to choose from various paper styles, including Normal (the default), Sepia (aged paper) and Night (high contrast).

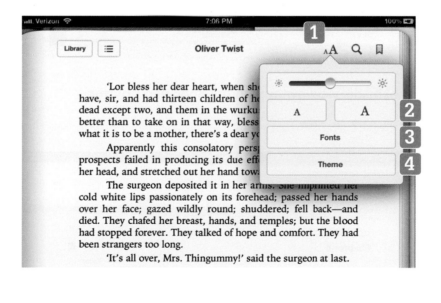

! ALERT: You might notice a short lag when you increase or decrease the type size, especially for longer ebooks.

? DID YOU KNOW?
You can turn your iPad into a dedicated ebook reader by engaging the Full Screen option under Themes. This setting removes the booklike interface around the pages and maximises your reading area.

Set and use bookmarks

You can bookmark individual pages of your ebooks and then return to these pages at any time in the future. You don't need to mark your place as you read, though; iBooks remembers where you stopped reading.

1 From any page of the ebook, tap the third button in the upper right corner, the one that looks like a ribbon.

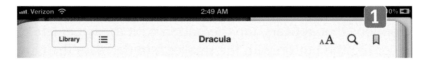

2 Notice that the icon turns into a red ribbon bookmark.

3 To jump to a bookmark, open the table of contents by tapping the button with the list icon.

4 Switch to Bookmarks view by tapping the Bookmarks button.

5 Choose a bookmark to view.

HOT TIP: Any ebook can have any number of bookmarks.

11 Getting oriented with Maps

Introduction

In countless movies and TV shows, characters wake up and ask where they are. Obviously these people don't own iPads, or else they do and they don't know how to use Maps. The Maps app in your iPad can tell you just where you are, and it can give you directions to almost anywhere. All you need is an Internet connection.

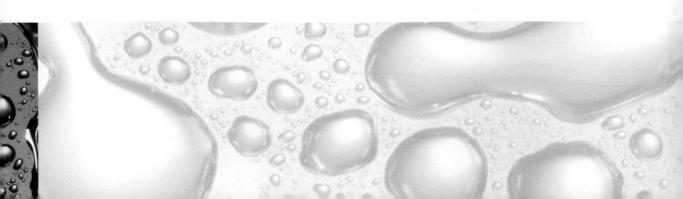

Find your location on the map

Your iPad can identify its physical location and display this information on the map in the Maps app. Assuming that you and your iPad are travelling together, you can see exactly where you are in the world.

1 In Settings, tap the Location Services item. Then, in the list of Location Services options, tap the On/Off switch for Location Services if this feature is currently disabled. You should also tap the On/Off switch for Maps if this feature is currently disabled.

2 Press the Home button to return to the Home screen, and then tap the Maps icon to launch Maps.

3 Maps displays your iPad's current location with a blue dot. At the top of the Maps interface, tap the icon that looks like a pointer until the compass appears. (You might need to tap this icon twice.)

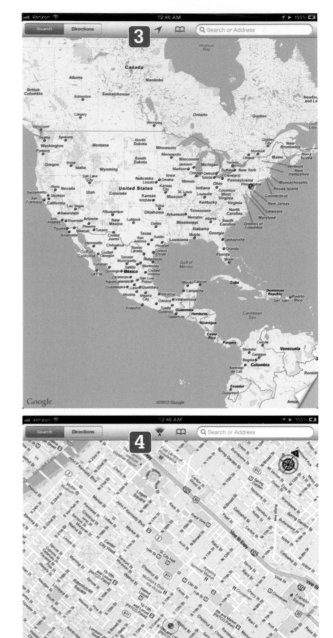

4 Take your iPad for a walk, and watch the map turn as you do. Tap the pointer icon one more time to hide the compass.

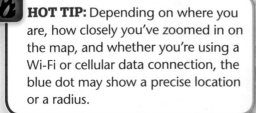

HOT TIP: Depending on where you are, how closely you've zoomed in on the map, and whether you're using a Wi-Fi or cellular data connection, the blue dot may show a precise location or a radius.

Navigate the map

Your iPad comes with a big display, but the world around you is bigger still. At times it helps to see a wide geographical area to get an idea of the distance from one place to another or to find a certain location. Other times you need to zoom in close to see the names of streets and so on. And you'll probably want to pan the map to see what's beyond the edges of the screen. Doing any of this is literally just a walk with your fingers.

1 To zoom out on the map, tap the map with two fingers at the same time, or touch the map with two fingers and move them closer together. To zoom in on the map, double-tap the map with one finger, or touch the map with two fingers and move them farther apart.

2 To pan the map, touch the map with one finger, and then drag your finger across the screen.

? DID YOU KNOW?

If you pan the map so that you don't see your blue marker anywhere on screen, tap the pointer icon once or twice. The map reorients itself to your iPad's current location (without affecting the current zoom level).

Search for a location

The Maps app has two modes: Search and Directions. The buttons for these modes appear at the top of the interface, on the left. When you're in Search mode, the search field appears at the top on the right.

1 Make sure you're in Search mode by tapping the Search button along the top.

2 Tap the search field. The virtual keyboard appears. You may also see a list of recent searches. If what you were about to enter is already in the Recents list, just tap its entry. If you don't find what you need in the Recents list, enter a search term: an address, a well-known location or a destination type.

3 Tap the Search key to continue.

4 Maps drops one or more red pins onto the map. Each pin represents a match from your search. Tap the head of a pin to see basic details about this place.

? DID YOU KNOW?

Maps enables you to search by address, of course, but you can also search by the name of an establishment or a famous landmark. You can even search by destination types such as bookstores, museums, tube stops and pubs.

🔥 HOT TIP: To remove the red pins, tap the search field again, and then tap its X icon.

Mark a location with a pin

You don't need to search for a location to drop a pin on the map. In fact, all you need is your finger.

1 In Maps, hold down your finger on the map until a purple pin appears.

2 To move the purple pin to a different location, drag it across the map with your finger, or repeat Step 1 on a different place on the map.

3 To remove the purple pin entirely, tap it (if necessary), and then tap its blue information button. In the information box that appears, tap Remove Pin.

? DID YOU KNOW?
You can have only one purple pin at a time.

Find more information about a location

Maps can give you detailed information about almost any pinned location.

1 On the map, tap the head of a pin.

2 Tap the blue information button that appears.

3 Read the information box.

HOT TIP: To close the info box, tap anywhere outside it.

Switch to Street View

Maps' Street View feature puts you 'on the street,' as it were, to give you a better idea of the location's surroundings. Not all locations have Street View, but many urban areas are quite well covered.

1 On the map, tap the head of a pin, and tap the red Street View button to switch to Street View for this location.

2 View the street.

> ⚠️ **ALERT:** Street View is amazingly cool, but don't count on it for complete accuracy. It doesn't give you a live feed of what's currently happening on the street. In fact, the photos in Street View might be many years old.

> 🔥 **HOT TIP:** You can drag Street View with your finger to see what else is nearby.

3 To pan Street View, hold your finger on the map, and drag your finger in any direction.

4 To 'walk down the street,' find the street indicator, and tap the arrow.

5 To return to the map, tap the location finder in the lower right corner.

? **DID YOU KNOW?**

Certain websites that offer Street View won't work in Safari on your iPad because these sites deliver Street View inside Flash applications, which iPad doesn't support. But this doesn't affect your ability to use Street View in the Maps app.

Get directions to anywhere from anywhere

The Maps app's Directions mode gives you turn-by-turn directions for finding almost any location. If you want to use your iPad's current location as the starting point, make sure that you've enabled Location Services for Maps; see 'Find your location on the map' at the beginning of this chapter for more information.

1 In Maps, tap the Directions button at the top of the interface.

2 Tap the field for the starting location, and enter the address or place-name of your starting point. Choose *Current Location* (if necessary) to use your iPad's current coordinates.

3 Tap the destination field, and then type the address or name of the destination. You don't need to be exact; you can type the name of a town or city, but doing so limits your ability to find a specific house on a specific street.

4 Tap Search on the keyboard. Maps computes a route between the points.

5 Near the bottom of the interface, find a bar of controls for the mode of transport: by car, by public transportation or by walking. The default is by car. Tap any other mode to get a new route.

6 If you're using public transportation, tap the button with the clock icon to choose your transit times.

7 Tap the Start button.

ALERT: The Maps app's directions don't take into account detours, recent construction, and so on. Always defer to traffic signs and the conditions on the road if you receive contradictory information.

DID YOU KNOW? Another way to get directions is to search for a location, tap its pin, tap the blue information button that appears, and then tap Directions To Here or Directions From Here.

8 Go through the legs of the journey step by step by tapping the arrow buttons on the right side of the bar. To return to the controls for the modes of transport, tap the left-arrow button until you return to the first leg of the journey, and then tap the left arrow one more time.

Share a location

When your mates don't know how to find your new flat, you can send them the location any number of ways.

1 Tap a pin on the map.

2 Tap the blue information button that appears.

3 Tap Share Location. A menu appears, asking if you want to share the location by email, instant message or tweet.

HOT TIP: When you share by email, you can send the location to multiple recipients at the same time.

SEE ALSO: To tweet, you need a Twitter account. For more information about Twitter, see Chapter 6.

4 If you choose email, your iPad launches the Mail app, opens a new email, and inserts the address details into the body text. Fill in the email recipient, and send the email.

5 If you choose instant message, your iPad launches the Messages app and attaches the address details to a new instant message. Select the recipient, and send the message.

6 If you choose to tweet, your iPad attaches the address details to a new tweet. Type any additional text, and send.

Bookmark a location

Bookmarking a location makes it easy to find in the future.

1 Tap a pin.

2 Tap the blue information button in the pin heading.

3 Tap the Add to Bookmarks button.

HOT TIP: You can bookmark the same location more than once. Just give each bookmark a different name.

4 In the Add Bookmark box that opens, tap Save. If you like, you can edit the name of the bookmark first.

Find a location from a bookmark

Once you bookmark a location, you can display it on the map at any time.

1 At the top of the map, tap the icon of the open book.

2 In the list that opens, tap the Bookmarks button if it isn't already selected.

3 Tap a bookmarked location. The map displays this location.

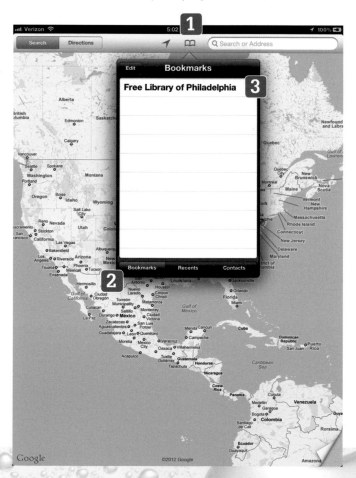

HOT TIP: Likewise, you can find a recent destination or a contact by tapping the Recent or Contacts button, respectively, and then choosing the desired item from the list.

12 Caring for your contacts

Introduction

Networking isn't a dirty word. Where would civilisation be without it? If you want to share the latest news or spread a bit of gossip, you need friends, family, associates, and so on. And once you have a couple people, it's only for the sake of convenience that you'd want to collect them in a single, tidy list. That list in your iPad is the Contacts app, and this chapter shows you how to use it.

Add a new contact

The more contacts you have, the better off you'll be, so why not add a few new ones today?

1 On the Home screen, tap the Contacts icon. The Contacts app launches.

2 The All Contacts list on the left shows your contacts in alphabetical order. To add a new contact, tap the plus sign (+) at the bottom of this list.

3 A blank entry for a new contact appears. Fill in the fields with as much information as you like. You don't need to fill in everything now.

4 To see additional fields, tap the green button to the left of the category that you want to expand.

5 When you're finished, tap the Done button at the top right of the contact record.

HOT TIP: One of the great things about your contacts list is that many of your iPad's apps can access it. You can address emails, send instant messages and make video calls from the information that you add to Contacts.

Assign a photo to a contact

Your list of contacts provides names, addresses, phone numbers, and so on, but what about photos? You can take any photo from your iPad and assign it to any contact in your list. You should probably choose a photo of the person, but there's nothing stopping you from using another sort of picture to represent one of your relatives (but only if they have a sense of humour).

1 If necessary, choose a contact, and tap the Edit button.

2 Tap the Add Photo field at the top left of a contact record.

3 From the menu that appears, tap Choose Photo, and then choose the photo that you want to use.

HOT TIP: If you're assigning a photo to yourself, tap Take Photo to use your Camera app.

4 Now move and scale the photo so that only the contact's face is showing. Use the stretch gesture to make the photo larger, and drag the photo to position it in the Choose Photo window. If necessary, use the squeeze gesture to make the photo smaller.

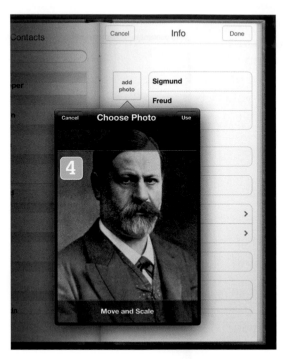

5 Tap Use. Contacts places the photo in the contact record.

6 Tap Done.

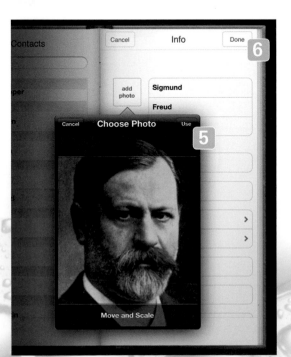

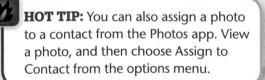

HOT TIP: You can also assign a photo to a contact from the Photos app. View a photo, and then choose Assign to Contact from the options menu.

Search your contacts list

If you tend to make a lot of contacts, you might find the search function useful.

1 Tap the search field at the top of the All Contacts list, and enter the name or other information that you wish to find. As you type, Contacts filters the list to show matching records only.

2 In the filtered list, tap a contact to view the full record.

HOT TIP: To clear the search field, tap its X icon.

Edit a contact

People move, change jobs, and get married. When they do, it's time to edit your contacts.

1 From the All Contacts list, select the contact to edit, and then tap the Edit button at the bottom of the contact record.

2 Fill in or edit any field of the record by tapping the field and typing (or retyping) the information.

3 To delete the information in a filled field without replacing it with updated information, tap the red button to its left, and then tap the Delete button that appears.

4 When you're finished, tap Done.

HOT TIP: To jump to a specific letter in your contacts list, tap the letter in the index tab down the left side of the interface.

HOT TIP: To edit the contact's photo, tap the Edit button beneath the current photo.

Delete a contact

Deleting a contact is just a tap away.

1 From the All Contacts list, choose the contact that you want to delete.

2 Tap the Edit button.

3 Scroll to the bottom of the contact record, and tap the Delete Contact button.

4 A confirmation box appears. Tap Delete to delete the contact.

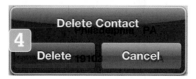

HOT TIP: What if you delete someone and realise later that you made a mistake? If you think that you might need to recover a contact in the future, just edit the name so that it starts with the letter X or Z. It might look a little strange, but at least all your borderline cases appear together in your contacts list.

Share a contact

This feature makes forwarding someone's contact information a breeze.

1 From the All Contacts list, choose the contact that you want to share.

2 Tap the Share Contact button. A menu appears, asking if you want to share the contact by email or instant message.

3 If you choose email, the iPad launches the Mail app and attaches the contact information as a VCF card. Address the email, and send it off.

4 If you choose an instant message, the iPad launches the Messages app and attaches the contact information as a VCF card. Choose your recipient, and send your message.

All Contacts

Q Search

E

F

Adrian **Foley**

Sigmund **Freud**

G

Greta **Garbo**

J

Mik **Jones**

M

Adrian **McNeil**

R

Grigori **Rasputin**

W

Herbert George **Wells**   **1**

Z

Thomas **Zachary**

Herbert George **Wells**

"H.G."

notes

Share Contact Using:

Email   **3**

Message

4

Share Contact   **2**

Edit

WHAT DOES THIS MEAN?

VCF: A commonly used file format for sharing contact information.

Add a contact from a VCF card

When someone sends you a VCF card, you can easily add the person in the card to your contact list.

1 In the email or message, tap and hold your finger on the VCF icon until a box appears with detailed information and options at the bottom.

2 Tap the Create New Contact button.

3 Add any additional information to the new record that you like.

4 When you're finished, tap Done, and then tap on a blank area of the screen to close the VCF box.

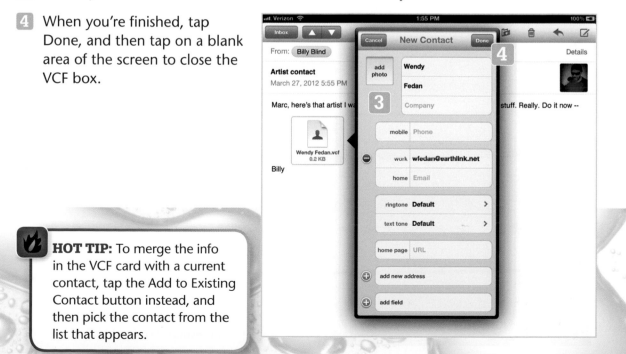

HOT TIP: To merge the info in the VCF card with a current contact, tap the Add to Existing Contact button instead, and then pick the contact from the list that appears.

Locate a contact on the map

If you've supplied an address for a contact, you can find this location in the Maps app with a single tap from Contacts.

1 From the All Contacts list, choose the contact that you want to find.

2 Tap the address.

3 See your contact's location on the map in the Maps app.

HOT TIP: When you're in the Maps app, you can find a contact on the map by typing the contact's name in the search field and then choosing this contact from the suggestions list.

13 Staying organised with Calendar

Introduction

Certain philosophers and even some scientists are of the opinion that time does not exist, which our too-busy lives would seem to bear out. But time problems are often just scheduling problems, and scheduling problems are no problem at all when you use the Calendar app on your iPad. Calendar looks and works like an appointment book, but one that you can easily search and modify – and one that can remind you to go to your meeting, call your mum on her birthday and pick up dinner on the way home. In this chapter, you learn how to use Calendar. You can't miss its icon; it's the one that shows the current date.

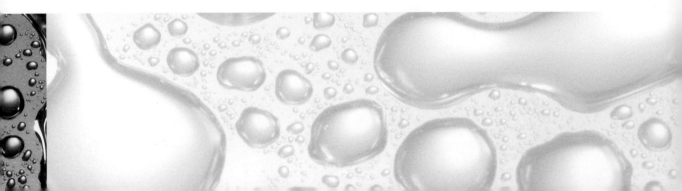

Explore the different calendar views

You can view the calendar for a day, a week, a month, a year or as a list of scheduled events. Tap an event to see its details.

 From the Home screen, click the Calendar icon. Your iPad launches Calendar.

2 Tap Day. In the middle of the list of the day's events, you find a thin bar with a red marker, which shows you where you are in your day. Tap an event to see its details.

3 Drag along the timeline at the bottom of the screen to show a different date.

4 To return to the current day, tap the Today button.

5 Tap Week to see the events for the current week. Tap an event to see its details in abbreviated form.

6 Tap Month for the monthly view. Tap an event to see its details in an abbreviated form.

? DID YOU KNOW?

The timeline and the Today button appear in all Calendar views, and they work much the same as they do in Day view. For example, in Month view, dragging your finger along the timeline switches quickly among months, and tapping Today returns you to the current month.

7 Tap Year for the yearly view. Highlighted dates have at least one event scheduled. Tap the date to go to Day view for that particular day.

8 Tap the List button to show upcoming appointments. Tap any event in the list to see your schedule for that day, and then tap an event in the daily schedule on that day to see its details.

Add an event

To schedule an engagement in Calendar, you add a new event. Each event is a collection of details: its name, its start time, its end time, and so on, along with a space for comments or notes. After you enter this information, Calendar displays the event under each of its views.

1 In Calendar, switch to the day of the event. If it's far in the future, go to Year view, and tap the date.

2 Tap the plus sign in the lower right corner of the screen.

3 In the Add Event box that appears, enter a title and, optionally, a location. Not all events have a particular location.

4 To enter the start and end times, tap the corresponding field. The Start & End box opens, with Starts highlighted.

? DID YOU KNOW?
No matter how you choose to review your schedule, your events appear exactly where you wrote them in.

? DID YOU KNOW?
You can sync your Calendar events with iCloud or iTunes.

5 Use the dial controls to set the date, hour and minute of the start of the event. If you need to change the time zone, tap the Time Zone control.

6 By default, Calendar sets the end time to one hour later. If this time is correct, just leave it as it is. If not, tap Ends, and then use the dial controls to set the appropriate time.

7 Tap Done to finish. The Add Event box shows the correct start and end times.

HOT TIP: Calendar suggests start and end times for the event. If these are correct, you do not need to enter a different set of times.

HOT TIP: Switch among calendars or create calendars of your own by tapping the Calendars button in the upper left corner of the Calendar interface.

8 Set the Repeat option if the event occurs at a regular interval. For step-by-step instructions, see 'Set an event to repeat' later in this chapter.

9 Under Invitees, you can choose to push invitations to this event to any of the people in your contacts list. (Likewise, your contacts can push invitations to you.) You and your recipients must have accounts on a network that supports Calendar invitations, such as iCloud.

10 Set the Alert option if you want your iPad to remind you about this event. For step-by-step instructions, see 'Set an alert to remind you of an event' later in this chapter.

11 Under Calendar, choose the calendar to use to schedule the event. The Calendar app gives you separate calendars for work and home.

12 Under Availability, choose whether you are free or busy for the duration of this event. If you receive an invitation to some other event that causes a scheduling conflict with this one, your availability determines the priority of your time.

13 To add a Web address that provides more information about the event, tap the URL field.

14 To add a comment about the event, tap the Notes field.

15 Tap Done. Calendar adds the event to your schedule.

? DID YOU KNOW?

If you add birthdays to your contacts in the Contacts app, these dates appear in Calendar under the special Birthdays calendar.

Edit an event

You can change the title, date, time or any other detail of a scheduled event. For example, you can change *Lunch with Bill* to *Dinner with Bill* to accommodate Bill's frantic schedule.

1 Tap the scheduled event and, if you're in Week or Month view, tap the Edit button.

2 In the Edit box that appears, tap any event detail that you need to change, and then either type the desired text or make a new choice.

3 Tap Done to save your changes.

? DID YOU KNOW?

If you change the date or time of the event, Calendar moves the event listing.

Delete an event

Schedules often change and events get cancelled – especially when you're dealing with Bill (from the previous task). You can delete any event as the need arises.

1 Tap the event and, if you're in Week or Month view, tap the Edit button that appears.

2 In the Edit box, tap Delete Event.

3 A confirmation appears. Tap Delete Event once again. Calendar removes the event from your schedule.

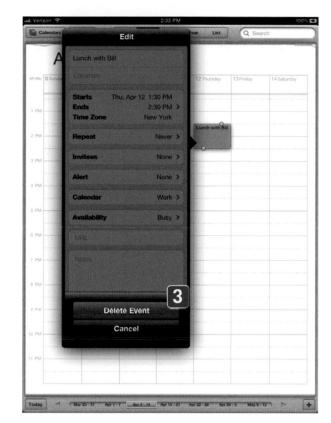

HOT TIP: When you delete a repeating event, you can choose to delete the upcoming engagement or the entire repeating sequence.

Set an event to repeat

Some events occur on a regular basis – your yoga class, your sales meeting. You can set up an event to repeat on this interval.

1 Add or edit an event, and tap Repeat in the Add Event or Edit box.

2 In the list of options that appears, select the appropriate interval, and tap the Done button.

HOT TIP: In any calendar view, the repeating event occurs on its interval indefinitely, unless you specifically choose an end date.

3 The display reverts to Add Event or Edit. Tap the new End Repeat option under Repeat.

4 In the End Repeat box, you can set the date upon which the repeating event ends, or you can set it to repeat indefinitely. Dial in or select the appropriate choice, and then tap Done.

5 Tap Done in the Add Event or Edit box.

Set an alert to remind you of an event

Calendar is great for keeping you organised. But on days when your schedule looks like air traffic control, Calendar by itself might not be enough. If you'd prefer a friendly reminder that a can't-miss engagement is coming up, Calendar can double as your personal assistant. When the time arrives for the alert, Calendar plays a sound, and you see a text reminder on the screen.

1 Add or edit an event, and tap the Alert button in the Add Event or Edit box.

2 In the list of choices that appears, choose when Calendar should alert you about the event.

3 Tap Done. The display reverts to the Add Event or Edit box.

HOT TIP: You can change the sound of the alert under Options > General > Sounds > Calendar Alerts.

4 Notice the Second Alert option; tap it to set a second reminder, and then tap Done. For example, you can set the first alert to 15 minutes before the event and the second reminder to 5 minutes before.

5 Tap Done in the Add Event or Edit box.

Set up an all-day event

Some all-day events are fun. Others are like a migraine headache. But Calendar makes no such distinctions and dutifully blocks out the time in your schedule.

1 While setting up or editing the times of your event under Start & End, tap to engage the All-day switch.

2 Now simply choose the day or days.

3 Tap Done.

4 In Calendar, look for the heading at the top of the day, which displays the title of the all-day event.

? DID YOU KNOW?

If you have a sequence of all-day events, such as your upcoming and well-deserved holiday, set the start day to the beginning of the sequence and the end day to its end. This way, you don't need to create separate all-day events for each individual day.

Search your events

As with most iPad apps, Calendar offers a search feature. You can search for a person's name, a location or some keyword that pertains to the event.

1 Tap the search field in the upper right of the Calendar interface, and enter a search term. Calendar displays a list of matching events.

2 To display the details of any event, tap its entry in the list.

HOT TIP: To clear the search field, tap its X icon.

Subscribe to a calendar

Some online services provide lists of dates – holidays, historical and so on – that you can load into Calendar. Your iPad displays information about these dates as they come up in your schedule.

1 In Safari, visit www.icalshare.com.

2 Search for something interesting.

3 Tap a calendar in the results.

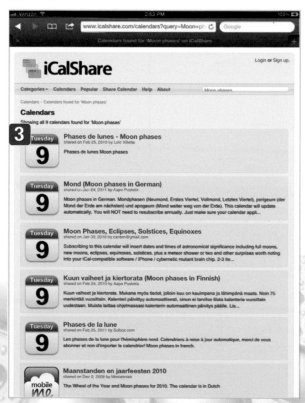

 ALERT: Make sure you pick a calendar that is compatible with the Calendar app. On this particular site, you can tell by the calendar's icon, which resembles the icon of your Calendar app.

4 Tap the Subscribe to Calendar button, and confirm if necessary.

5 To see the dates that this calendar contains, launch Calendar, tap the Calendars button in the upper left corner and, in the list of calendars that appears, make sure that this calendar shows a tick mark beside it.

HOT TIP: To unsubscribe to a calendar, go to Settings > Mail, Contacts, Calendars, and look under the Accounts heading for the Subscribed Calendars field. Click this field to see a list of all subscribed calendars. Then click the calendar to open its information box, and tap the Delete Account button.

14 Taking notes

Introduction

When it comes to ideas, you simply never know when inspiration will strike. Thoughts come and go and sometimes slip by, unless you carry a notebook around, but why bother with that when you're toting an iPad? The Notes app looks and works much like a standard yellow tablet (the paper kind). Each page or *note* is like a piece of paper for text. You can leaf through the sheets one at a time – or you can instantly find a particular word or phrase. Just try to do that with a stack of paper.

Review a note

Reviewing your notes is as simple as launching the Notes app.

1 On the Home screen, tap the Notes icon.

2 Tap the Notes button.

3 Choose a note from the list that appears. Your iPad displays the note in the main Notes interface.

4 Read the note.

? DID YOU KNOW?

A note may contain more text than fits on a single screen, so to read the entire text of a long note, you might need to scroll.

Add a new note

Your iPad can hold a vast number of notes. Each note consumes a tiny bit of storage space, but the amount is so small that, for all practical purposes, your iPad's note tablet will never run out of pages, so feel free to add as many as you need.

1 Tap the plus sign in the upper right corner of the Notes interface. Notes creates a new note.

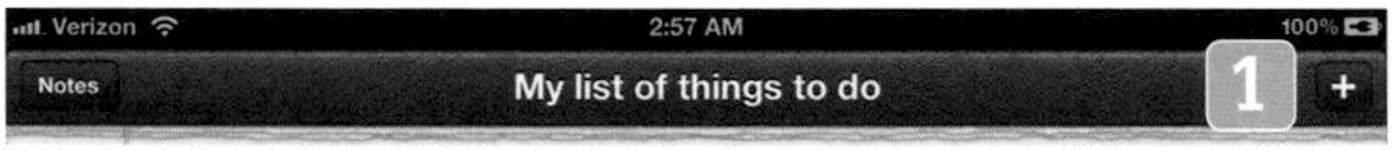
Verizon
2:57 AM
100%
Notes
My list of things to do
1
+

2 Type the text of the note.

Verizon
2:58 AM
100%
Notes
Guest list
+
Today
Apr 1 2:56 AM
Guest list
Barack
Michelle
Joe
Jill
Bill Maher
Bill Moyers
Susannah
Mr David Fedan
Wendy Fedan
Billy
Denzel
Lenny
Ben
Frederego
Freud
2

HOT TIP: To change the typeface of the text in your notes, tick an option under Settings > Notes. Changing the typeface affects all the text in all your notes.

DID YOU KNOW?
You can sync your notes with iCloud. Just make sure you set up all your devices to receive synced notes.

Edit a note

You can edit a note at any time.

1 Tap a line in the content of a note.

2 Type your changes.

Delete a note

After you've completed every task on your to-do list, it's time to send your note to the garbage.

1 If necessary, open the note that you wish to delete, and hide the virtual keyboard if it is open. Then tap the Trash icon along the bottom of the screen. The Delete Note button appears.

2 Tap Delete Note. The note is as good as gone.

Delete Note

? DID YOU KNOW?

Instead of deleting a note, consider recycling. I'm being totally serious. Just empty out the lines of your to-do list except for the title. This way, depending on how you sync, you don't end up with multiple to-do lists.

Email a note

Storing notes in your iPad is great – until someone in Belgium needs to see what you wrote. Email to the rescue!

1. If necessary, open the note that you wish to send, and tap the icon immediately to the left of the trashcan. A menu of choices appears.

2. Tap Email.

3. Notes launches the Mail app, creates a new email, and puts the text of your note in the body of the email. Just enter a recipient and send.

HOT TIP: To print a note, follow the same procedure, but tap Print instead of Email in Step 3. Just keep in mind that, to print from your iPad, you need to be able to connect to your printer wirelessly, and you must also download the appropriate third-party printing app from the App Store.

Browse through your notes

You can flip through the pages of your notepad just as you would a non-virtual one.

1 If necessary, hide the virtual keyboard.

2 To browse to the previous page in Notes, tap the left-arrow icon at the bottom of the screen.

3 To browse to the next page in Notes, tap the right-arrow icon.

HOT TIP: To jump to a specific note, open the Notes list, and choose the note that you want to see.

Search your notes

When you need to find something in one of your notes but you can't recall which note it's in, you can perform an easy search.

1 Tap the Notes button to open the list of notes.

2 Tap the search field at the top of the list, and type in a search term. As you type, your iPad filters the notes to show only those containing the text that you typed.

3 Tap a note to see its full text.

HOT TIP: To return to the full list of notes, clear the search field by tapping its X icon.

15 Using accessibility features

Introduction

Your iPad comes with a number of accessibility features to deliver the best possible experience for people with vision impairment, hearing impairment or limited physical abilities. One such feature is VoiceOver, which instructs the iPad to read the text on the screen. Another is Zoom, which increases the magnification of icons and text. What you might not realise, though, is that accessibility can be useful for everyone. For example, if your Home button stops working, you can enable the AssistiveTouch feature and put a Home button on the screen.

Use VoiceOver

The VoiceOver feature enables your iPad to read to you. The voice speaks the names of buttons and other interface elements as well as the text in emails and documents. When you enable VoiceOver, the gestures that you use to operate your iPad change slightly. If you're used to standard iPad controls, you might feel disoriented at first, but a little practice goes a long way.

1 From Settings, tap the General item.

2 Tap Accessibility. You may need to scroll down to see it.

> **!** **ALERT:** Don't be startled when you turn on VoiceOver and the iPad begins speaking.

3 Tap VoiceOver.

4 Tap the On/Off switch to engage VoiceOver. If this is the first time that you have used VoiceOver, an alert box appears, indicating that VoiceOver changes the gestures that you use to control the iPad. Double-tap the OK button to continue.

5 Tap one of the sample blocks of text. A black border appears around it, and the voice reads the words. Tap a control to highlight it, and then double-tap it to activate it. To scroll, drag three fingers on the screen instead of just one.

6 Engage the Speak Hints setting to hear more information about what is happening in the iPad, such as when the screen changes. Not all items provide extra information with Speak Hints enabled.

Change the speaking rate

You can control the speed at which the voice talks. A setting of around 20 per cent is roughly the speed of normal speech.

1 Under Settings > Accessibility > VoiceOver, with VoiceOver enabled, tap the Speaking Rate slider to select it.

2 Double-tap the slider, but on the second tap, hold your finger down; don't remove it from the screen.

3 Drag your finger to the left or right to decrease or increase the speed of the voice.

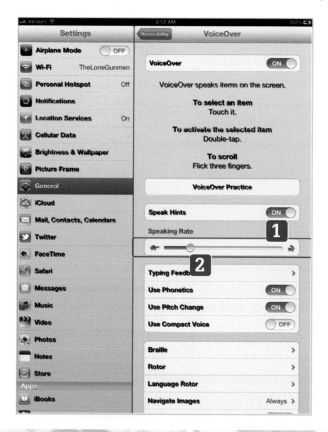

HOT TIP: You might want to start out with a slower voice, especially if you are new to the iPad. As you become more accustomed to working with it, feel free to increase the pace.

Use Zoom

The Zoom feature magnifies the screen.

1 From Settings, tab the General item.

2 Tap Accessibility, and then tap Zoom.

3 In the list of Zoom options, tap the On/Off switch to engage Zoom:

- To switch between magnified and unmagnified view, double-tap with three fingers, and release your fingers on the second tap.

- To increase or decrease the magnification level, double-tap with three fingers, but on the second tap, keep your fingers on the screen. Then drag your fingers up to increase magnification or down to decrease magnification.

- To scroll the screen, drag with three fingers.

HOT TIP: When you need to find an app on the Home screen, double-tap with three fingers to zoom out. Access the app by its icon, and then double-tap again with three fingers to zoom back in.

? DID YOU KNOW?

If you have trouble reading small type but don't want to magnify the entire screen, try the Large Text option under Settings > General > Accessibility > Large Text.

Use White on Black

The White on Black feature inverts the colours of the display for better contrast in apps like Mail. Hence, black text on a white background becomes white text on a black background.

1 From Settings, tap the General item.

2 Tap Accessibility.

3 Tap the White on Black On/Off switch to engage this feature.

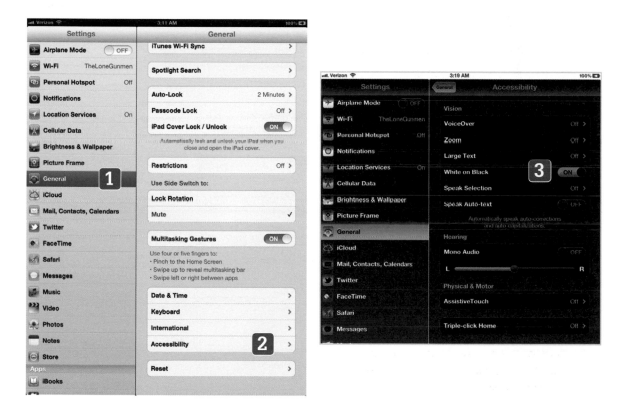

? **DID YOU KNOW?**

When White on Black is engaged, all the onscreen colours change, including the colours in photos and movies. You probably want to disengage White on Black when you aren't doing a lot of onscreen reading.

Convert audio to mono

By default, audio output from your iPad is in stereo. However, to accommodate users with hearing in one ear only, you can change the audio output to mono.

1 From Settings, tab the General item.

2 Tap Accessibility.

3 Tap the Mono Audio On/Off switch to engage this feature.

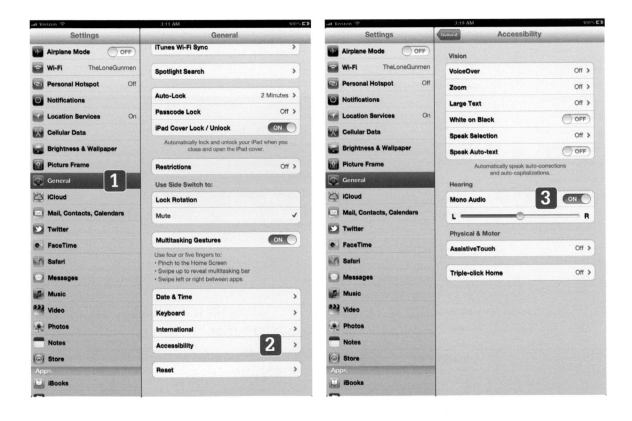

? DID YOU KNOW?

Stereo audio assigns different instruments or different parts of the sound to the left and right channels of the stereo image, which correspond to your left and right speakers or the left and right pods of your headset. Over speakers, stereo and mono might sound very similar to you, even if you hear in one ear only. But if you prefer to use a headset, you'll definitely miss the full range of sound in the audio unless you convert the stereo to mono.

Use AssistiveTouch

The AssistiveTouch feature enables you to control your iPad with a limited number of gestures or a compatible accessory like a joystick. For people who have trouble using the touch screen, AssistiveTouch provides a fantastic workaround.

1 From Settings, tap the General item.

2 Tap Accessibility.

3 Tap AssistiveTouch.

4 In the list of options that appears, tap the On/Off switch to engage AssistiveTouch. Your iPad places a round cursor in the lower right corner of the screen.

5 Drag the cursor around the screen to position it where it's most comfortable for you. When you need to perform a gesture, tap the cursor.

6 Choose from the menu that opens:

- **Gestures:** tap one of the icons to simulate a two-finger, three-finger, four-finger or five-finger gesture.
- **Device:** tap one of the icons to simulate the physical controls on the iPad, including the volume and the orientation of the screen.
- **Home:** tap this icon to simulate a single click of the Home button.
- **Favorites:** choose a favourite gesture from the menu that appears.

7 Return from the submenus by tapping the arrow icon in the middle, or close the menu by tapping anywhere outside it.

? DID YOU KNOW?
If the physical buttons on your iPad wear out, you can use AssistiveTouch to simulate their functions via the touch screen.

HOT TIP: The Favorites menu includes multiple slots for custom gestures that you record on the touch screen. To record a gesture, look under Settings > General > Accessibility > AssistiveTouch > Create New Gesture.

Triple-click the Home button to set accessibility features

You might recall from Chapter 9 that you can press or click the Home button more than once in succession to issue commands to your iPad. For example, on the Home screen, clicking twice calls up a bar of recently used apps. Normally, triple-clicking the Home button does nothing, but you can instruct your iPad to engage or disengage your favourite accessibility feature on triple-click to save you constant trips to the Settings app.

1 From Settings, tap the General item.

2 Tap Accessibility.

3 Under Accessibility, tap Triple-click Home.

4 From the list of options that appears, choose the accessibility feature that you want to control with triple-click. Choose Off to do nothing, or choose Ask to see a menu of options whenever you triple-click.

ALERT: The Ask option doesn't include AssistiveTouch.

16 Getting more out of Settings

Introduction

For the number of times you've gone into the Settings app, you should know by now how useful it is. Yet this book hasn't shown you a third of all that you can find in there. In this last chapter, I call your attention to a smattering of these for your greater enjoyment of the iPad experience.

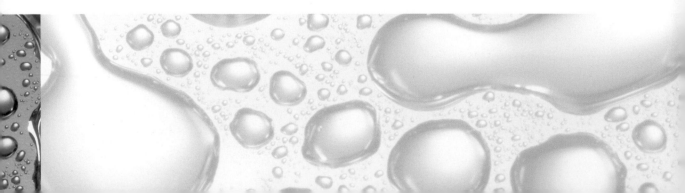

Use Airplane Mode

When you travel on a commercial flight, you usually need to turn off your wireless devices, and your iPad is nothing if not a wireless device. But you don't need to lose your videos and tunes for that red-eye to Moscow, when you need them the most. Simply set your iPad for Airplane Mode to shut off your iPad's wireless signals.

 From the Home screen, tap Settings.

Find the On/Off switch for Airplane Mode at the top of the list of settings. To engage Airplane Mode, tap this switch. You can tell that Airplane Mode is active when you see an aircraft icon in the upper left corner of the screen.

ALERT: Don't forget to disengage Airplane Mode once you're back on terra firma.

See your iPad's stats

Your iPad tracks a number of different stats: the number of photos, videos and songs stored; the amount of storage space that you've used; the amount of storage space that remains; and so on. You can access these stats whenever you like.

1 In Settings, tap General.

2 Tap the About item in the list of general settings.

3 Read the information that appears.

HOT TIP: Another way to find some of the same information is to sync your iPad with iTunes on a computer.

Check cellular data usage

If you connect to the Internet by a cellular data plan, you can find out just how much data you've sent and received – which is helpful indeed if your plan comes with a monthly limit.

1 In Settings, tap Cellular Data.

2 Tap the View Account button in the list of options that appears, and follow the onscreen instructions.

HOT TIP: You can change your cellular data plan and edit your payment information by following the same steps.

Change sound alerts

When certain actions occur, such as when you send mail or when you tap a key on the keyboard, the iPad plays a particular sound. You can change the default sounds to any number of built-in options, and you can even buy new sounds if you get tired of all the old ones. For a few features, you can turn off the sound entirely.

1 In Settings, tap General.

2 Tap Sounds in the list that appears.

3 Tap the sound that you wish to change, and then choose a new sound from the menu that opens.

4 To turn off a sound entirely, tap its On/Off switch.

HOT TIP: The global volume control appears as a slider at the top of the Sounds screen. Dragging this slider affects the volume level for all apps, movies, music, and so on.

Use Location Services

Many apps, including Maps, make use of your current location to provide special features. These features work only when you engage Location Services.

1 In Settings, tap the Location Services item.

2 Tap the On/Off switch to engage or disengage this feature.

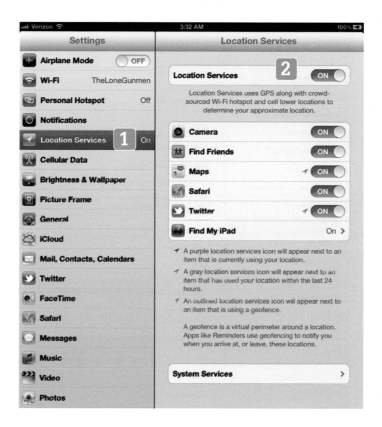

HOT TIP: You can also apply Location Services selectively to the apps that use it. Find an app in the list under Settings > Location Services, and then tap its On/Off switch to engage or disengage Location Services for that particular app.

Set the date and time

When you connect your iPad to Wi-Fi or a cellular carrier, the iPad can determine the date and time on its own. But if you need to change the date and time and you don't have an Internet connection, you can make these changes manually.

1 In Settings, tap the General item.

2 Tap the Date & Time option. You might need to scroll the list to see it.

HOT TIP: If you prefer the 24-hour clock instead of 12 hours with AM and PM, tap the On/Off switch next to the 24-Hour Time option.

3 If the Set Automatically feature is engaged and you have Internet connectivity, there is nothing further for you to do; but if you disengage the Set Automatically feature by tapping its On/Off switch, further options appear.

4 If necessary, tap Time Zone to select the correct zone. A screen appears for you to identify your location; type the city or region of your time zone.

5 Tap Set Date & Time to dial in the correct date and time. The dial switches change depending on whether you tap the date field or the time field.

Set international preferences

The iPad offers international preferences with regard to language, keyboard and region. The choices within these categories may differ as you make your selections. For example, selecting French for the language changes the choices within the Region preference.

1 In Settings, tap the General item.

2 Tap the International option. You may need to scroll the list to see it.

ALERT: Changing the language for the fun of it might end up backfiring on you, since you might not be able to read the onscreen text well enough to get back into the language settings. Look for the icons! They will keep you on track.

3 To change the language, tap Language, and choose your preference from the Language box that appears. Your iPad takes a moment to reset itself. It may appear to turn off, but it is merely in Sleep mode; just press the Home button to resume operation in the new language set.

4 To change the keyboard, tap Keyboards. Tap the name of the current keyboard to see a list of all international options. Choose one to change your keyboard preference.

5 To change the way that your iPad formats dates, times, telephone numbers, and so on, tap Region Format, and choose from the list of regions.

6 To change the calendar type, tap Calendar, and choose from the list of calendars that appears. Western countries generally use the Gregorian calendar.

Top Ten iPad Problems Solved

Problem 1: The iPad isn't responding

Your iPad is a computer, and all computers get stuck every once in a while. If your iPad doesn't respond at all to your taps, try turning it off and then turning it on.

1 Turn off the iPad by holding down the On/Off, Sleep/Wake button until the screen shows the red slider switch.

2 Move the slider on the screen to complete the shutdown.

3 Wait a few minutes, and then hold down the On/Off, Sleep/Wake button until you see the Apple logo.

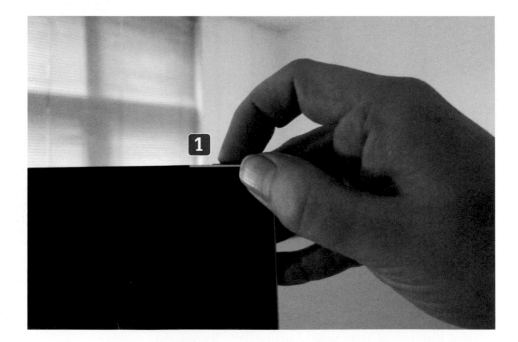

HOT TIP: If you notice that your iPad gets stuck whenever you use a certain app, delete the app if you can. If one of the core apps is causing the problem, contact the store where you purchased the iPad for help.

DID YOU KNOW?
It's a good idea to shut down the iPad occasionally anyway, even if there are no performance problems.

Problem 2: The iPad isn't responding at all – not even to restart it

This occurrence is rare, and hopefully you will never come across it. However, if the iPad is completely unresponsive to the point that you can't even turn it off, then you need to perform a system reset.

1 Simultaneously press and hold down the On/Off, Sleep/Wake button and the Home button for 20–30 seconds, until you see the Apple logo on the screen. Then let go of the buttons.

2 Wait a few moments until the Home screen appears. Your iPad should now be ready to go.

ALERT: Resetting your iPad might cause you to lose some data, but you can sync with iTunes on your computer after the reset to reinstall your media and apps. And if you're an iCloud user, depending on your iCloud configuration, you might not even need to do that.

Problem 3: I need to erase all my data and files

If you're selling or giving away your iPad, or if you just want to start afresh, you can restore the iPad to its factory conditions.

1 From Settings, tap the General item, and then tap the Reset button. You'll need to scroll all the way to the bottom of the general options list to see it.

2 Tap Erase All Content and Settings.

3 Tap Erase in the Erase iPad message that appears.

ALERT: Make sure to back up all the media and data that you want to keep before you erase your iPad by syncing to iTunes on your computer or engaging the iCloud service.

HOT TIP: The other Reset buttons restore different aspects of your iPad's configuration to factory conditions without erasing your media files. If you don't need to wipe your iPad completely clean, you might consider one of these options instead.

Problem 4: I can't connect to the Internet

Not having an Internet connection when you expect one can be frustrating. Try the following fixes.

1 In Settings, check whether Airplane Mode is engaged. If it is, tap its On/Off switch to disengage this feature.

2 If you connect to the Internet using Wi-Fi, tap the Wi-Fi item under Settings. Make sure that Wi-Fi is engaged and that you're connected to a network.

3 If you connect to the Internet using a cellular data service, check the signal strength by the number of bars in the upper left of the screen. You might be in a location that has poor coverage. Change locations, if you can, and see if you get a better reception.

 HOT TIP: Moving physically closer to the source of the Wi-Fi router (or removing any obstacles between the Wi-Fi router and your iPad) can help to resolve connection problems.

Problem 5: Some websites aren't working correctly

The likely culprit is either JavaScript or Flash. You can enable JavaScript support in Safari settings, but Flash is a different and thornier issue. Apple doesn't support the Flash media format on mobile devices, including the iPad, and there are no signs that this policy will change. In fact, recent developments in the online world suggest that Flash is becoming an obsolete format. If your favourite site uses Flash extensively, you simply can't view this content on your iPad without altering or *jailbreaking* your iPad's operating system – and thus invalidating your factory warranty and preventing System Reset from working.

1 To engage JavaScript, go to Settings, and tap the Safari item. Then tap the On/Off switch next to the JavaScript option.

2 If the site uses Flash content, you see a message on the page that asks you to download the Adobe Flash plug-in, but if you attempt to download this plug-in, a page on the Adobe site tells you that Flash is incompatible with your mobile device. You can't view a site with Flash on your iPad, but you can visit this site on a desktop computer.

DID YOU KNOW?

Some sites with lots of Flash content – including YouTube – provide separate, Apple-mobile-friendly versions. This is why you visit m.youtube.com in this book instead of www.youtube.com. Maybe your favourite Flash site also has a mobile version that works better with your Apple device.

Problem 6: The iPad displays the wrong time

Your iPad determines the local time by your location setting. If you see the wrong time, your iPad might think that it's in a different time zone, which you can easily correct.

1 In Settings, tap the General item, and then tap the Date & Time option in the list of settings that appears. You might need to scroll the list to find this setting.

2 If Set Automatically is set to On, set it to Off by tapping the On/Off switch.

3 Tap the Time Zone button, and change the time zone to your location.

HOT TIP: When Set Automatically is set to On, your iPad ought to keep accurate time. If the clock starts acting strangely, you might just need to log on to your Internet connection for a couple of minutes or, failing that, restart your iPad.

Problem 7: All the emails I send say 'Sent from my iPad'

Your iPad automatically inserts a brief piece of text or *signature* at the end of your emails, and the default signature line is, 'Sent from my iPad'. You can change this signature to whatever you like, or you can remove it entirely.

1 In Settings, tap the Mail, Contacts, Calendars item, and then tap the Signature option in the list of settings that appears.

2 Type your preferred signature in the field that appears, or erase the text in the field to remove the signature line from your emails.

HOT TIP: Your signature can contain multiple lines. Just tap the Return key at the end of each line.

Problem 8: The iPad sorts my contacts list by first name instead of last name

A setting determines how the iPad sorts your contacts list. If you prefer to sort your contacts by last name, simply change the setting.

1 In Settings, tap the Mail, Contacts, Calendars item, and then tap the Sort Order option in the list of settings that appears.

2 Tap the Last, First option.

? DID YOU KNOW?

The Display Order setting determines how your iPad displays the names of the people in your contacts. This setting doesn't need to match the sort order. So, for example, you can sort your contacts list by Last, First but display your contacts by First, Last.

Problem 9: The virtual keyboard is difficult to use

If you find that typing on your iPad's virtual keyboard for any length of time is tiresome, you're not the only one. Apple understands this problem well. You might try the following workarounds.

1 Enable and use the Dictation feature. Under Settings > General, tap Keyboard, and then tap the On/Off switch next to Dictation if it is set to Off. See 'Dictate instead of type' in Chapter 1 for more information.

2 Enable the Auto-Capitalization, Auto-Correction, Check Spelling, and '.' shortcut settings under Settings > General > Keyboard. (To use the '.' shortcut, double-tap the spacebar key to insert a full stop and space.)

3 Change the layout of the keyboard so that half of it appears on the left side of the screen and half of it appears on the right. You might find this layout more comfortable for two-handed typing. Hold down the key in the bottom right of the virtual keyboard, and choose Split from the menu that appears. To restore the keyboard to its default layout, hold down the same key, and choose Dock and Merge from the menu.

4 Consider purchasing the Apple Wireless Keyboard, which connects to your iPad by Bluetooth. See 'Connect a Bluetooth device' in Chapter 1 for more information.

? DID YOU KNOW?

You can replace the standard English keyboard with an international version. Look under Settings > General > Keyboard > International Keyboards > Add New Keyboard, and choose the layout that works best with the language that you need to type.

Problem 10: I erased an app or media file by mistake

To err is human. To erase iPad content is forgivable and, thankfully, recoverable.

1 If you use iTunes to sync, connect your iPad to your computer. As long as your computer retains a copy of the app or media, syncing restores the missing content to your iPad.

2 If you use iCloud to sync, go to the App Store, the iBookstore, or iTunes on your iPad, and tap the Purchased category. (In iTunes, tap the View button in the upper left corner of the screen to view purchased music, movies or TV shows.) Then just download the app or media file again.

ALERT: If you use iCloud to sync, you might need to sync with iTunes anyway to restore media that iCloud doesn't normally support, such as songs that you obtained outside the iTunes Store. Alternatively, you can subscribe to Apple's iTunes Match service, which makes iCloud available for your entire music library, not just the music that you bought from the iTunes Store. To subscribe to iTunes Match, launch iTunes on your computer, and choose Store > Turn On iTunes Match from the main menu.

Spot Goes to the Farm

Eric Hill

PUFFIN

Are they in the barn?

Are they in the stable?

Who's that hiding behind the bush?

And who's that hiding in the straw?

Hurry up, Spot!

Spot, get out of

the pond!

Quick,
Spot,
follow me!

Here they are!

Come on, Spot! There's nothing in there.

Did Dad

show you the piglets, Spot?

Yes, and then <u>I</u> found some kittens to show Dad!

PUFFIN BOOKS

Published by the Penguin Group: London, New York,
Australia, Canada, India, Ireland, New Zealand and South Africa
Penguin Books Ltd, Registered Offices:
80 Strand, London WC2R 0RL, England

puffinbooks.com

First published by William Heinemann Ltd, 1987
Published in Puffin Books 1990

37 39 40 38 36

Printed and bound in Singapore

ISBN 978–0140–50932–8